A Great Russian Tone-Poet
SCRIABIN

BY

A. EAGLEFIELD HULL

MUS. DOC. (OXON.)

EDITOR OF "THE MONTHLY MUSICAL RECORD"

WITH 165 MUSICAL ILLUSTRATIONS AND 4 PLATES

LONDON

KEGAN PAUL, TRENCH, TRUBNER & Co., Ltd.

BROADWAY HOUSE, 68–74 CARTER LANE, E.C.

1916

ALEXANDER SCRIABIN
(1914)

[*Frontispiece*

CONTENTS

FOREWORD

THE author lays no claim to have written a full biography of Scriabin. The material to hand was not sufficient for this; and many channels of information were closed by the great European war. Scriabin domiciled in at least three countries—Russia, Switzerland, and Belgium; and toured in eight foreign lands. One of his aims has been to furnish an account of some of the most interesting and important experiments which have ever been made in musical art. Scriabin's activities were many-sided and far-reaching; and, in one respect at least, he may be said to have himself consummated the possibilities of their application.

Many people have wondered where the purely physical development of music on the lines adopted by Debussy and others was leading us; Scriabin shows us its fullest possibilities—*and its limitations.* He gives us a completely new system of harmony; he abolishes the major and minor modes; he annihilates modulation and chromatic inflection; he abandons all key-signatures; and finally applies his ideas to the most modern scale we have reached so far, i.e. the "Duodecuple." Moreover, at the time of his death he was experimenting with the unification of the various arts of sound, light, and bodily movement (*mimique*); and, as if all this were not enough, wove a system of theosophy into the art of his latest period. Although probably too much account has been taken of the latter, yet surely the sum-total of Scriabin's work has brought about an artistic revolution unequalled in the whole history of the arts.

As one of the chief aims of the book is the further spreading of the knowledge of Scriabin's work, only those biographical details are supplied which have a direct bearing on his creations. Much of his life-story had to be pieced together bit by bit; and half the charm in writing the book was the dovetailing of English, French, and Russian newspaper reports, articles from periodicals, etc., into the very incomplete sketches of Mr. Eugen Gunst. Some of it is mere conjecture—a dangerous plan in biography in general—but reasonable enough when only applied to such minor details as humdrum Conservatoire courses, etc.

The author has been greatly indebted to the writings of Mr. Leon Sabanieff as well as Mr. Eugen Gunst; to his correspondent Miss Ellen von Tideböhl of Moscow; and also to his friend Mr. W. Bray for much help with translations, etc. These acknowledgments apply mainly to Chapters III to VI. For the rest—analysis, technique, and æsthetics—he takes the full responsibility on his own shoulders. The "first person" has been used with appreciations and criticisms in order to prevent the reader from accepting the opinions as dogmatic or in any way final. Any æsthetic musical criticism which claims to be more than a personal expression is to his mind hollow and insincere. Especially would this be the case with so recent a composer as Scriabin. There must be the same general consensus of approval of the later works of Scriabin by musicians, as there is with the earlier works, before we can clearly decide his place amongst the greatest in music.

At present there is certain to be a small minority of the older musicians to whom *all* modern music is distasteful. For these, it is hoped that the present book may at least place them into a position with Scriabin's music similar to that of the Russian General regarding Wagner's music. He "didn't like it, but he wasn't afraid of it."

The Russian dates have been used throughout for all events except the London Concerts. To arrive at the correct Western dates, add thirteen days to the given date. No apology is made for the spelling of Russian names. It is quite impossible to write some of them correctly in English. No two writers render them alike, and even Russian scholars differ.

There remains to be acknowledged the great help so readily given by the composer's friend and English host Mr. Kling, of Messrs. Chester and Co., Great Marlborough Street, W. The portraits of Scriabin are produced by his kind permission.

A. E. H.

SCRIABIN

I

INTRODUCTION

HAVE you ever considered what a truly wonderful and deeply mystical thing a musical sound is? If you sprinkle some light sand on a pianoforte lid or, better still, on a specially arranged vibration plate, and strike a complete chord, the sand will begin to dance about and finally settle down into a beautiful geometrical pattern; strike another chord and the gyrating sand will finally dispose itself into a set of four roses or something equally interesting. Now thump the piano lid with your fist and the sand will heap itself up anyhow. That represents the difference between musical sound and noise.

But perhaps the most mystical part of sound and light too is that there is no such material at all. Both are *vibration* interpreted differently. That is all.

If you were to start the full organ in Westminster Abbey going by some mechanical process and go away closing the Abbey to everyone, but leaving the organ going at full blast, the Abbey would be soundless. Why? Because to complete the Sound mystery, you must have a participant who will be a mental interpreter before you obtain any sound at all.

This brings to mind that wonderful little "Corti's organ"—a sort of piano keyboard—inside everyone's ear, the hundred little keys of which are flying up and down recording sensitory impressions all day long!

Then what a wonderful thing is the sympathetic vibration of sound—a close analogy to the resultants of two adjacent complementary colours in painting! That Sèvres vase there on my mantelpiece might be broken without any physical contact whatsoever—just by standing on the other side of the room and playing the right note on a violin.

Further—we know that no musical note is single or isolated, but that every apparently single sound has numberless little satellites, some of which we cannot detect, but all there nevertheless. These upper "partial sounds" can be reinforced or weakened by the different qualities of instruments, by the arrangements of harmony, and by many other means.

Small wonder then that this mystery has proved a siren from time to time to draw men's minds from musical *art* to the *science* of musical sound, and thence back again to a possible combination of the two. A veritable *ignis fatuus* it has indeed proved hitherto, for musical harmony as we know it was surely never evolved from acoustic laws, but on purely æsthetic lines.

The Right Honourable Arthur J. Balfour, addressing the International Musical Congress in London at their Fourth Annual Congress, said: "Of all the arts, Music seems to be connected more intimately than any other with dry scientific facts. You can state in mathematical physics, certain important truths with which music is intimately connected. But I do not believe that out of the mathematical theory of the scale or of the chords, or of the theory of harmony, anything in the nature of a true musical æsthetic can ever be deduced." This was in 1911, and all the leading musicians present cordially agreed with him.

. . . . . .

Yet all the time a great new tone-poet was working in Russia on these very lines which had been voted so impossible. Scriabin derived all harmony from "Nature's harmonic chord," and thus carried the Science of Sound triumphantly into the regions of Art. But he attempted more than this.

What shall we say of the wonders of Light and Colour? Photography has reached undreamt-of stages, and artists have analysed and tabulated the chromatic rays, the principal relation of tones, their complementary colours and resultant tones, but no union has yet been effected between the Scientific knowledge and a system of Æsthetics. Again, Light, like Sound, is no concrete object, but just a fleeting impression recorded in various ways through the mind of the individual receiver.

Truly little do we know about the Science of Colour; yet here is a musical genius with the amazing temerity to propose a union between these two great mystic forces, Light and Sound. Certainly a record of the works and doings of such a man is worth attempting.

II

THE MUSICAL AWAKENING IN RUSSIA

"*Everything has a father.*"
Russian Saying.

ANY attempt to appreciate Scriabin—much more to understand him thoroughly—without a knowledge of the growth of Art-music in Russia would end in failure to seize many of the leading characteristics of his work.

Many critics have divided music by Russian composers into two clear divisions, distinguishing the purely Russian art like Mussorgsky's from that of the eclectic composer like Tchaikovsky. But the Russian when clad in Western clothes cannot help being Russian, just as much as when he wears the caftan and *chapan*. There are hundreds of passages in Tchaikovsky's works which only a Russian could have written; and only Russia could have produced a nature so peculiarly endowed as Tchaikovsky's. So it is with Scriabin. Although he was trained on the purely eclectic system, which has been more particularly the chief feature of the Moscow Conservatoire, rather than that of the Russian Northern capital, yet he was essentially Russian by nature, and, as a matter of course, shows this in his music.

. . . . . .

Russia, that land of extremes, that mighty empire which spreads itself out vastly over two continents, that nation of numberless races populating its wealthy cities, navigating its mighty rivers, and spreading themselves out in settlements over its boundless plains, has at least two national characteristics which permeates its utmost extent—from the Baltic shores in the North to the southern Russian confines of the Caucasus, from the sunny slopes of the Urals to the bleak Kirghiz wastes. And these two characteristics which bind all these races in one are that wonderful gift of imagination which begets and retains for ages the stories of the *vodyano* (rivergods), the *lesi* (woodsprites), the humanised animals, the ugly old witch, Baba-Yaga (the sound of whose name is enough to quieten the crying child with chilling fear), the miraculous hens, the midnight dances, and so on; and their marvellous love of folk-music, song and dance which has ever held as firm a hold on these vast races. The traditional songs sung and danced to the *gusslee* and the *balalaika* embrace the whole of national life, transmuting the misery of their present condition into beautiful dreams of the past, and aspirations for the future. Ethnological and geographical conditions thread their music with strands of every hue. In the inclement regions of the North the songs have a long-suffering melancholy note, but where Russia touches the fairy East, their melodies are gracious and tender, evocatory of the Sun, and infused with languor.

But more than any other race, it is the Slavs—

that purest of all the Russian stocks—who sing. In the government of Novgorod, of Moscovy and Little Russia, the Slavs sing at their work, at their play, at their religious festivals, at the rites of the seasons; they celebrate musically all the events of their lives—birth, love, marriage, and death; trouble, sorrow, good fortune, and parting; the rain, the river, the sky, and all Nature herself; they sing in solo, in chorus, in legend, in *byliny*, in dirge, in dances; in songs of work and travel and in the home. They are always deeply saturated with the poetry of the race from which they spring. What immense possibilities are open to a race who have thus retained through the ages the pristine freshness of the great human springs.

Small wonder that the minds of such musical composers as Stravinsky, Rébikoff, and Scriabin fly with almost feminine intuition to the very fount of the race, when primitive man was apparently as unsullied as Nature herself. Truly enough there is a deep gulf fixed between musical Art and the Folk-music; but the imagination and the poetry of the *moujik* comes out just as surely in the mysticism and originality of the twentieth-century *intelligentsia*.

As an art Music was slow to rise in Russia, and even then its late advent had to be brought about from outside. This exotic impetus was a thing the Russian musical composer never seems to have forgiven and periodically resents; for their excitingly full musical history, though short and recent, is the story of a continual and exaggerated " harking back to the people." First it was Glinka—then Cui—then Mussorgsky; and both Tchaikovsky and Scriabin were accused from time to time of being "not sufficiently Russian."[1] But Nationalism in Music can easily be carried too far. So can Exoticism: witness England.

. . . . . .

There was and still is a sort of Art-music of great antiquity in Russia. I refer to the unison chants of the Orthodox Church, directly descending from the Greek Christians,—that purest form of the ancient Christian Church, polluted neither by temporal ambition nor mercenary desire. The pure and pristine state of their Church music is of supreme value to the Russian musical composers, for it has kept them away from the hard grip of the limited major and minor scales.

. . . . . .

A short sketch of the rise of Russian secular musical art is necessary before we begin our study of Scriabin. In former times, music as a profane art was little estimated in Russia. In the Middle Ages the Church banned it entirely; and even as late as the sixteenth century a canon forbade it. An ancient mural painting depicts the tortures specially reserved in hell for the musician. In the seventeenth century a general destruction of all musical instruments was ordained, and even at the present day, no instruments are used in the Russian Church service. Many people attribute the wonderful sonority of the Russian voices, and their

[1] See pages 54, 55.

remarkable ability of retaining the pitch, to this invariable custom of unaccompanied vocal singing.

In the eighteenth century, both the Czarina Anne and the Czarina Elizabeth were keen music-lovers, but it was only the foreign musicians who were encouraged by them. The first attempts at operas with Russian subjects and written in the Russian spirit were made by Khatchin (his *Tanioucha* was produced in 1756), Fomin (*Aniouta* in 1772 and *The Miller* in 1779), Matinsky (*Gostiny Dvor*, "the Market-place"), Cavos, and Titoff. Cavos was a Venetian who settled in Russia for forty-five years (1795 to 1840) and caught the Slav spirit to a remarkable extent. Then came Vertovsky's *Askold* (1835) and other pieces. These tentative efforts were brought to a head by Glinka's *Life for the Czar* in 1836. This opera was the foundation-stone of Russian music. After it, two courses only were open to the Russian composers—either a complete severance from the foreign art in style and matter, or else a spiritual change of the contents in the foreign moulds. After the manner of revolutions, the more violent course was at first adopted. Glinka set the ball rolling, but he was not strong enough nor were the circumstances sufficiently favourable for a complete departure. Before his time nothing but Italian music (and that in its decline) had entered Russia. All other European music was a closed book to them.

When exotic influences did finally enter Russia it was chiefly through the Romanticists—Weber, Berlioz, and Liszt. When Glinka visited Berlin in

1832 and heard Weber's *Freischutz*, he was absolutely stunned; and when, a few days later, he witnessed Beethoven's *Fidelio*, his lot was cast. In his own operas, Weberian influences continually crop up; but this is all the more excusable when we remember the spell which Weber threw even over Berlioz and Wagner. Weber's love of Oriental subjects would have a special appeal for Glinka, who, in his first opera, was twenty-five years ahead of Wagner in his *Rienzi*. When the French master Berlioz visited Petrograd and Moscow in 1847, he was fêted like a monarch. The Russian school owes an incalculable debt to this remarkable genius, especially in the development of orchestration. Still more do they owe to that great reformer of musical construction—Franz Liszt—the creator of the modern symphonic style. From him they learnt richness of harmony, deftness in handling themes, and sonority of orchestral *timbre*.

. . . . . .

We will break off our operatic story, to notice a fact of great importance to our study of Scriabin. In 1804 Clementi, the famous pianist and piano manufacturer, brought with him to Petrograd from his London piano warehouse a pale melancholy Irish youth, awkward and shy, to "show off" his pianos to the fashionable Russian nobles and ladies. John Field, for that was his name, played the Fugues of Bach and Handel to them in a remarkable way, and so great an impression did he make in the Northern capital that he soon discovered he could do something better there than "show off pianos." Consequently, when Clementi left he settled down in Petrograd and became the fashionable teacher, pianist, and composer. His compositions number 7 *Concertos*,[1] a *Quintet* and *Rondo* for Piano and Strings, some Variations on a Russian air for four hands, 4 *Sonatas*, a *Fantasy on a Polish theme*, a *Scotch Rondo*, *Two English Airs varied*, and 20 *Nocturnes*.

He was the veritable inventor of the Nocturne. In these *Poésies intimes* of such simple charm and naïve grace we find the very essence of Chopin's idylls and eclogues; and from Chopin the mantle fell directly on to the shoulders of Scriabin. In the notice on Field in Grove's Dictionary, Mr. Dannreuther writes: "Both as a composer and as a player, Chopin, and with him all modern pianists, are deeply indebted to Field. The form of Chopin's Nocturnes, the kind of emotion embodied therein, the type of melody and its graceful embellishments, the peculiar, waving accompaniments in widespread chords with their vaguely prolonged sound resting on the pedals, all this and much more we owe to Field." Field stayed in Petrograd nearly twenty years, and then went on to Moscow, where he was even more successful. There he died, and was buried in January, 1837. Here in Field, the Irishman, we find indeed a powerful exotic influence transplanted for good into Russian music.

In opera, however, the national tendency became

[1] One of the Concertos (the 5th) is entitled "L'incendie par l'orage."

very marked. Glinka's work was carried on by Dargomijsky—a great Russian reformer of dramatic musical declamation. His aims reached far beyond those of Wagner, approximating closely to those of Debussy's *Pelléas et Mélisande* twenty years later. His music is simple, sober, and direct, and follows the text with remarkable closeness and fidelity. Moreover, he did not use a specially prepared *libretto*, but took Pushkin's prose as it stood. His orchestration too could be very picturesque on occasion (see his tone-poem *Baba Jaga*), and he raised the national dance, the *Kosatchok*, to an artistic realisation.

After him came that remarkable Petrograd group known as "the Five": Borodin, Cui, Balakireff, Mussorgsky, and Rimsky-Korsakoff. They aimed at, and indeed achieved, the establishment of the opera built up on the foundation so well laid by Glinka and Dargomijsky, and they transferred the musical freedom thus gained into absolute music. The style and traditions of the Haydn, Mozart, and Beethoven forms were resolutely cast off. The work was of immense importance to Russian music. Later on Rimsky-Korsakoff seceded from the group when he felt that the isolation of national music might be carried too far.

The Petrograd Conservatoire of Music was founded in 1861 by Anton Rubinstein, who remained its Principal for nine years. At first thoroughly eclectic, it gradually came under the influence of "the Five." Rimsky-Korsakoff was appointed

Professor in 1871, and Asanchevsky, one of Mussorgsky's earliest musical friends, became Principal in 1874. The work there has now become more eclectic again, and numbers of magnificently equipped pianists and composers leave its portals crowned with their medals.

At Moscow things have always been much more eclectic. Influences come continually from all quarters, from the East as well as from the West. The Moscow Conservatoire of Music was founded in 1864 by Nicholas Rubinstein, and its ideal has always been much more cosmopolitan. Tchaikovsky—a truly eclectic musician—became Principal in 1876. Taneieff followed, and Safonoff succeeded him in 1889, and retired in 1906. The present Principal is Ivanoff-Ippolitoff. The Moscow group of composers has always been a brilliant one, including such musicians as Arensky, Conus, Rachmaninoff, Glière, Ilyinsky, Kalinikoff, Kashkin, Koreschenko, Siloti, Sokoloff, and Spendiaroff.

Opinions are much divided on the question of Nationalism in Music and its foundation on the Folk-song; but the history of musical art teaches us that music is a universal art, and that whilst it gains much by reverting from time to time to the original stock, yet it cannot isolate itself for long without an irreparable loss to itself. At first sight, many people may not hear the national strain in the music of Scriabin, for he is singularly free from idiom. But if the following sketch does not succeed in revealing ample evidences of this "strangely unknown people with their incredible other-worldliness, their broad tolerant charity, their freedom from chilly conventions, their joyous neglect of the hustle and fussiness of Western life, their deep faith, their child-like superstitions, and the glorious promise of their future," it will be the fault of the hastiness of my sketch; for it is all clearly stamped on his life and works.

III

THE EXPOSITION: SCRIABIN'S PARENTAGE AND CHILDHOOD

Moscow at the end of 1871 was little different from the Moscow of to-day, and was, in all external aspects, practically the same picturesque capital of Oriental design and grandeur which Napoleon viewed from the Sparrow Hills in 1812. The tourist arriving at the Smolensky Terminus in Moscow at the present day, after driving through the picturesque quarters in the neighbourhood of the Triumphalnaya, the crude log cottages surrounded by gay gardens, and the wood and plaster houses bright with white, blue, yellow, and pink walls, with roofs of dark green and deep crimson, and then through the winding Tverskaya, its thick-walled habitations fairly bristling with great overhanging spouts, may be a little disappointed as he comes out on the modern up-to-date shops in the Nikolskaya and the fashionable hotels of the Grand Square.

But let him wander for half a minute down the Ilyinka, and he will find himself again amongst these quaint alleys and courtyards of old Moscow; and in the middle too of a veritable babel of Eastern tongues, for these are the old street markets

(*Gostiny Dvor*) which continue right up to and round the walls of the entire *Kitai Gorod.* Or let him take but a few steps westwards, and pass through the *Triotsky Vorot* (*Trinity Gate*) into the marvellous Kremlin itself—and he has stepped straight out of the twentieth century into the Middle Ages.

No; other cities give way to progress and modern ideas, but Moscow the Golden, the Mother of the mighty Russian race, appears to go on for ever.

. . . . .

On the evening of Christmas Day, 1871, in Moscow, with the thermometer at 14° below zero, things looked particularly cheerless out in the long, crooked streets, covered with a deep snow. The thousands of bells so busy and joyous dring theu morning had ceased their glad tidings. The reddened sun, which had only shown itself for a few hours in the leaden sky, had suddenly disappeared. The cold atmosphere seemed scarcely yet to have settled down after such an unwonted agitation, even in this the "city of bells." Great snowflakes were still slowly and steadily floating down to earth. The quaint, almost bizarre outlines of the city, all covered with the enfolding mantle of snow, assumed as the great quiet of evening came on a feeling of weirdness and unreality. The homeward-bound traveller, dashing along silently in his fashionable *troika*, found his mind, like his body, becoming more and more benumbed with some undefinable sense of melancholy in the overhanging gloom.

It was only when some huge oaken door was flung open suddenly or a *dvornik* flashed his lantern across a storied courtyard, that the least suggestion of the universal cheerfulness and joyfulness of Christmas festivities and gladness was confirmed. Then the flying traveller caught sight of cosy fire-settles and domestic circles, hardly suspected under so forbidding and cold a covering.

Particularly in one home was there an atmosphere of unusual excitement and emotional glow. Bustle and hilarity were everywhere in this house. A queer lop-sided mansion of considerable size, evidently very old, it nestled in snowy hoods of irregular outline under the shadows of the massive towers of the Pokrovsky Barracks on the Kyriakoff estate.[1] The homestead belonged to Alexander Ivanovitch Scriabin, who came of an old aristocratic Russian family; aristocratic because in Russia this goes entirely by military rank, not as in England by civic titles, and Alexander Ivanovitch Scriabin had been a Colonel for many years in the army.

At his house on this Christmas night there was a full family gathering of six sons and one daughter. Something more than ordinary Christmas happiness and joy of family union was here; for the son Nicolas, a newly-fledged young lawyer from Saratoff, had brought his young wife to his parents' home for the Christmas holidays; and there at two o'clock in the afternoon of this very Christmas Day a son had been born to them. No wonder the pleasant kindly face of the young newly-dubbed "Aunt

[1] This estate no longer exists.

Luboff "[1] was aglow with excitement. The happy father was receiving congratulations and toasts were going all round.

The grandfather's soldierly instincts had been gratified by his eldest son following a military career. He was indeed attached to the neighbouring military settlement as tutor ; and so his second son Nicolas had been allowed to take a course of Jurisprudence at the Moscow University. Whilst still in his studentship he has met, admired, and loved a brilliant young pianist from Petrograd—Luboff Petrovna Stchetinin by name. Marriage followed closely on the heels of love; students' classes, and even " prospects " must wait. " They are always there," as the Russians say. The eager couple did not number forty years between them. The young pianist continued her classes at the Petrograd Conservatoire of Music, under the famous Leschetizsky,[2] and received in due time the Artistes' Gold Medal. Her husband meanwhile finished his jurisprudence at the University, and then the couple had settled down at Saratoff, where the husband opened practice as a lawyer, the wife continuing her musical work.

Saratoff (Tartar for " yellow sand ") is the largest city on the Volga, which is there two miles broad, and although five hundred miles from the mouth the river is already at sea-level. The population is

[1] Luboff, a favourite Christian name in Russia. English—Love.

[2] Leschetizsky was born of Polish parents in Lemberg in 1830. He was Professor at the Petrograd Conservatoire for many years, retiring in 1878.

an exceedingly varied one. Tartars jostle with Kalmucks and Cossacks from the Don and Kirghiz, with long flowing *chapans*, caught up with silk or leather girdles and round, pointed hats, add striking picturesque notes to the scene. There were too even then a large number of prosperous German colonies and a small English one.

In 1871 the young married couple had gone to spend Christmas with the older Scriabin family, who lived at Moscow, and here on this bleak Christmas Day of 1871 the future musical composer, Alexander Nicolas, was born, as we have narrated.

We can deduce no hard-and-fast rule defining the value of genealogy in art. The fathers of Handel and Rubens were both lawyers; Shakespeare's father and Dvorak's father were both butchers; the father of Michelangelo was Governor of the Castle of Capressi; whilst Mendelssohn's father was a wealthy banker, and Beethoven's a poor tenor singer in the Electoral Chapel at Bonn. On the other hand, John Sebastian Bach, Mozart, and our own Samuel Wesley all came of notable musical parentage.

The composer Scriabin's genealogy shows no marked musical traits on the male side; but although we know little about the Stchetinin family, it is obvious that the young mother possessed very unusual musical endowments and abilities. Alas; six months after the birth of the son destined to such great musical fame, the young mother developed an ominous cough. Tuberculosis was diagnosed. Undaunted, however, Luboff continued her musical activities in preparation for her concert work, her husband having again entered the Petrograd University. The illness, however, became more disquieting, and in September of the same year it was necessary for her to be taken abroad. They went to Arco, a small town beautifully situated on Lake Guarda, in the South Tyrol. Despite the excellent climate and all attention, the illness grew apace, and terminated fatally in April, 1873. They buried her there in Arco.

Such a disaster—one of the most terrible tragedies which can befall a man—can only be met, if at all, by a complete breaking with the old life. The newly-fledged lawyer returned to Petrograd, broke off his University studies, and determined on Consulate work in the East. He entered the Institute of Eastern Languages, and studied hard for two years, when he received his first post as *dragoman* (official interpreter and assistant consul) at the Russian Consulate in Constantinople. But so indefatigable a worker was not destined to remain long in any one post. He was soon appointed Consulate-Secretary at Betoly—then Vice-Consul, later on Consul, and finally he received the appointment of Chief Consul at Erzeroum.

Erzeroum was, and still is, a fortified city of great strength in Asiatic Turkey; it has a large Moslem and Armenian population of about 50,000. It is about midway between the Russian border and the River Euphrates, being 355 miles from Tortum Lake. It was captured by the Russians in 1829, but given back to Turkey a few months later by the Peace of Adrianople. During the war in 1877 it was unsuccessfully stormed, but came into Russian occupation the following year. It was shortly after this that Nicolas Scriabin was appointed. The post was doubtless an important one. The trade amounted to about £400,000 a year, exporting wheat, skins, furs, and tobacco. There were several European Consulates resident, also a Pasha, an Armenian Patriarch, and a Greek Bishop. At the very moment of writing (February, 1916), news comes that this great fortress has again fallen into the hands of the Russians (for the third time, for it had been ceded back to the Turks by the Treaty of Berlin). Although possessing a healthy climate, an atmosphere generally dry, and a splendid water supply, even at the present day the city has the unenviable reputation of being the most insanitary town in that most insanitary of countries—Armenia.

. . . . . .

Nicolas Scriabin retired from the Russian Consulate there in the "'eighties"; and, having had enough of life in the East, settled down at Lausanne, in Switzerland, where his son frequently visited him. He died there on December 24, 1914, only four months before the sudden death of the composer.

. . . . . .

To return to the Scriabins at Moscow in 1872—owing to the unsettled position of the bereaved husband, the motherless babe was first taken into his uncle's house at Moscow; and when three years old, he was removed to his grandmother's, where from this time all supervision of his education was undertaken by his maiden aunt, Luboff Alexandrovna Scriabin. Her tender care was the subject of the most touching affection on the part of the composer throughout his life.

Early signs of the young Alexander's unusual musical endowments were not slow in revealing themselves. When only five years old he would extemporise on the piano, though it was some time before he could *write* music. His acute ear and his musical memory were astonishing. A single hearing of any piece was sufficient to enable him to sit down and reproduce it exactly on the piano. In 1877, during the Russo-Turkish War, when the Ismailovsky Guards Regiment was leaving for the seat of war, the young boy was taken to the station to see his uncle off with the rest of the Guards. During the entraining, the band played a Quadrille, then very popular, called "The Snow-storm." On his return home, the five-year-old musician played the piece through on the piano from memory from beginning to end, greatly to the amazement of the family. Later on, when he heard his foster-mother play a *Gavotte*[1] by Bach, and the *Gondolier's Song*[2] by Mendelssohn, young Alexander, then a boy of eight, immediately sat down and reproduced them without a mistake.

[1] Probably one from the *French Suites*. Aunt Luboff must have been a well-taught pianist.

[2] *Songs without Words*. Book I, No. 6.

From his earliest age he showed an independent and inventive turn of mind, always disliking to imitate or copy anything exactly, but much preferring to take his own initiative. With him, no incentive to study was needed, for he was never happy unless he was doing something. Once, on seeing embroidery being done, he also wished to do some; and when canvas, thread, and frame were given to him he ignored the marked patterns and boldly worked out his own design.

From the age of eight years he composed a few simple pieces, and also developed a strong love for poetry, writing many short poems himself. He also amused himself a good deal by cutting things out of wood, and this inventive pastime even extended to the making of miniature pianos, in which he was particularly successful.

From a very early age his relatives took him frequently to the Imperial Moscow Opera House. Here from time to time he would hear some of the chief operas of the newly-formed Russian School—Glinka, Mussorgsky, Cui, Borodin—and the early works of Wagner. More frequently, as in the England of the "'eighties," the Italian composers would occupy the stage—Rossini, Donizetti, Bellini—with occasional performances of the French composers Gounod and Bizet's works.[1]

[1] Of late years the repertoire has been much enlarged. The Imperial Opera House in the season 1912–13 recorded 176 performances of 22 various operas, 11 by Russian composers (120 performances), and 11 by foreigners (56 performances). Tchaikovsky was the first on the list, as his operas were performed 32 times, and his ballets 15 times. The number of presentations by other composers was as follows: Rimsky-

The Imperial Opera House in Moscow is next to La Scala at Milan, the largest in the world. It has always possessed an excellent Chorus and Orchestra, and in addition to giving Grand Opera, also presents that special Russian form of art, the "ballet"—a combination of the finest music, dancing, and *mimique*. As at Petrograd every *employé* in the Opera is a Government *employé* and qualifies for a Government pension. It is the same with the Imperial Theatre of Drama. In Russia, actors and singers are rightly considered part of the national system of education.[1] The army officers receive special benefits at the Opera Houses.

At the Opera the elder Scriabin noticed that the young boy's ears were always much more occupied with the magical sounds of the orchestra than his eyes were concerned with the happenings on the stage. This tendency explains why, despite the preponderance of the operatic influence in Moscow, Scriabin developed entirely on non-operatic lines.

Korsakoff 27; Glinka 22; Mussorgsky 16; Rubinstein 17; Thomas 15; Gounod 12; Wagner 11; Bizet 9; Rachmaninoff 8; Verdi 6; Dargomisky 4; Massenet 3.

Zimin's Opera Company gave in the same season 265 performances of 31 operas, of which 15 were by Russian composers, 138 times, and 17 by foreigners, performed 133 times. Tchaikovsky was the most favoured as his operas were given 54 times. The number of operas by other composers was as follows: Rimsky-Korsakoff 49; Puccini 29; Verdi 21; Nougues 21; Bizet 19; Rubinstein 17; Leoncavallo 14; Strauss 10; Rébikoff 7; Gounod 5; Mascagni 5; Gretchaninoff 4; Mussorgsky and Lortzing, Massenet, D'Albert, 3 each.

[1] At the time of writing (February, 1916) the English Treasury has just withdrawn the whole of its insignificant grant to special musical training, amounting to about as much as the cost of the single firing of a gun of one of our big Dreadnoughts.

He was destined to be the composer of that purest form of music—instrumental music freed from all trammels of action, scenery, and even of words.[1] He wrote no vocal music at all.[2]

A purely dramatic turn, however, obsessed him in these early years. Thus, when a miniature folding theatre was bought for him, he scorned the idea of following the printed directions and would have naught to do with the given play, but staged his own pieces, dramatising in his own free way whatever stories he had been reading. One of his favourites was Gogul's "The Nose."[3] Nor did he stop here. He even wrote whole tragedies himself in prose and in poetry. Like another illustrious composer,[4] in his keen desire for the quintessence of drama, he had frequently killed off all his characters by the time he had reached the third act. "Auntie," he would exclaim, "I've no characters left to go on with." When thus occupied he would lose himself entirely, first jumping about and declaiming with outstretched arms, then sitting down and writing further.

Scriabin's early education seems to have been

[1] Later on, as we shall see, he attempted the unheard-of conjunction of colours, and even proposed odours.

[2] Excepting the "Choral Epilogue" to his First Symphony and the *ad lib.* Chorus parts to *Prometheus*, where the singers merely vocalise, however.

[3] Nicolas Gogul, the great national story writer, a brilliant satirist, "the Russian Dickens," was born in 1798. Gogul's influence on Russian musicians has been paramount. Glinka, Seroff, Mussorgsky, Solobieff, Stchurovsky, Tchaikovsky, Rimsky-Korsakoff, all wrote operas based on his fantastic stories. Glazunonoff wrote a Symphonic Prelude "In Memory of Gogul" in 1909.

[4] Richard Wagner.

much on the same lines as that of the little Tchaikovsky. In both, the stimulation of the imagination and the feeling for original creative work played a great part. In the middle and upper classes in Russia, owing to the constant intercourse between the children and the grown-up people, mental interests grow at a very early age.[1] These conditions of home life have a twofold result. On the one hand, a considerable amount of good accrues in the acquisition of knowledge itself and in the development of an impressionable nature; and on the other hand, the physical well-being often suffers. No Russian child of twelve would be satisfied with the little picture-books and stories (chiefly humorous) which are printed for English nurseries. He wants serious books and—*novels*.

Some such criticism might perhaps be levelled at the system of young Scriabin's upbringing. Certainly he ended in being a "thorough-going mystic." But his foster-parents cannot be said to have played any further part in influencing so obviously gifted a nature beyond giving his obvious inventive and musical gifts every opportunity of development. Except too for his sudden fatal malady Scriabin never suffered any serious illness.

. . . . . .

The father paid regular visits, in his vacations from his Consular duties at Betoly (and later on from Erzeroum) to see his little son at Moscow. There is a portrait of the father and son together taken in

[1] See N. Jarintzoff, *Russia: The Country of Extremes* (1914).

1883 on one of these occasions. The father, well built, very upright but rather under average stature, black hair, high forehead, small nose, lips a little full, chin firm but not protruding, a look of assurance and trustworthiness about the countenance. The son, a youth of eleven years, very proud of his new cadet's uniform, epaulettes, breast-chain, and belt. He had just been admitted into the Cadet's School attached to the military establishment at Podrovsky in the outskirts of the city, where one of his uncles was a tutor. In appearance the boy favours the father, who is there seated with the boy's hand placed affectionately on his shoulder. These Russian people know how to love well, and they know how to sustain parting. I can well imagine the picture was taken just before one of the many dreaded leave-takings prior to the father's return to his duties in the East. Sweet remembrances of past good times and hopes of more in the time to come help the boy to show a brave face to the future. So I read the young firm face.

. . . . . .

And there was always dear Aunt Luboff to go to for encouragement, for the boy seems to have been the dearest thing in her life. Then a time arrives when her watchful education and tender care must give way to sterner tasks and harder ways—to tutors, to school routine, and to the healthy stimulus of boy companions of his own age.

IV

FIRST SUBJECT: SCRIABIN'S STUDENTSHIP

"The boy is father of the man."

IN Russia, national service claims every man at any rate for some period of his life. In most cases education takes a special bent (especially if it is of military description) at an earlier age than in other countries. The Government offers to take charge of the sons of officers from the age of ten, to feed, clothe, and house them gratuitously. This continues until they are ready for the *junkers'* school, which corresponds to our Sandhurst.

In his tenth year, then, young Scriabin was placed in the 2nd Moscow Army Cadet Corps. Alexander did brilliantly at the Entrance Examination. He did not "live in" with the rest of the students, but remained at the house of his uncle, who was a tutor to the Corps. The youngster soon succeeded in winning the sympathy of teachers and students alike, and became a great favourite with his young companions, who would gather around to hear him play pieces on the piano, or recite some poetical effusion of his own. Though he seems to have had no leaning towards the science of war, he remained in the Cadet Corps for nearly nine years. All this time his musical talent was developing rapidly. His first piano lessons were taken privately from Professor G. A. Conus, and later on from Zvierieff, whilst musical theory was studied with the Principal, Taneieff. G. A. Conus was a Professor of Theory, Harmony and Orchestration, as well as of Pianoforte Playing at the Moscow Conservatoire, but Zvierieff was the Principal Professor of Piano Playing (Rachmaninoff was one of his pupils). Taneieff followed Tchaikovsky as Principal of the *Conservatoire* in 1882.

At that time Scriabin's foster-parents lived in a house in Zlatoustinsky Court. Hither Taneieff himself would often accompany the young boy home, for he was not allowed to go about alone. The streets of Moscow are literally overrun by the diminutive open cabs called *droshkys*, which go everywhere, even into the narrowest alleys. The driver—the *isvostshik*—belongs to a class which outvies the old London " cabby " in humour, carelessness, and irresponsibility. Moreover, even at the present day no police regulations prevail over these fiery Jehus, who swoop down on you at every corner. Once when going over the Kouznetz Bridge alone, young Scriabin was knocked down by a *droshky*, and his right collar-bone was broken.[1] Throughout the period of his convalescence, Alexander practised on the piano *with his left hand alone.*[2]

[1] Eugen Gunst in the Russian Journal *Rampa and Theezn* (Body and Soul) in 1914.

[2] This period of left-hand development may account in some measure for the extraordinary difficulty of the left-hand parts in many of his pieces. Certainly it explains the Op. 9, *Two Pieces for Left Hand alone.*

His passion for music seems to have gradually ousted his military studies, for the young boy composed day and night. Whilst doing so, he never liked to be left alone in the room, but always begged his fond aunt to sit up with him. She often remained thus with him far into the night. Private music lessons no longer sufficed for his needs. Whilst still continuing the Cadet courses, he was now fully entered as a student at the Moscow Conservatoire of Music. He studied in the Pianoforte class of Vassily Ivanovitch Safonoff, and in the Counterpoint class under Taneieff.[1]

It is time now to study the training for which the Moscow Music Conservatoire has long been justly famous. From 1885 Taneieff was Principal, but he resigned the Directorship in 1889 in favour of Safonoff. Taneieff, however, still continued his classes there, Composition and Counterpoint being his favourite subjects. The influence of this fine, broad-minded man, of such splendid and sound musicianship, on Scriabin was of inestimable benefit. Exceedingly modest by nature, a born teacher and a composer of great merit, Taneieff attracted to his cosy little house at Klin, in Demianovo, a large number of pupils; and many musicians and composers of great fame visited him there. His *Manual*

[1] Sergius Ivanovitch Taneieff was born in 1856 in the government of Vladimir. At the age of ten he entered the Moscow Conservatoire as a student under Lander. At the advice of Nicolas Rubinstein, he continued there under Hubert and Tchaikovsky. He took the Gold Medal for Piano-playing, and toured as a pianist. Tchaikovsky, having failed to induce Rimsky-Korsakoff to undertake the Directorship, offered it to Taneieff, even serving under him on the staff for a time.

SERGIUS IVANOVITCH TANEIEFF
(SCRIABIN'S TUTOR)

of Counterpoint, published in 1896, demonstrates his remarkable system of teaching Counterpoint by means of algebraical symbols. He takes Leonardo da Vinci's motto as the keystone for his work:

Nissuna humana investigatione si po dimandare vera scientia, s'essa non passa per le mattematiche dimostrationi.[1]

This conjunction of musical Counterpoint with Mathematics seems all the more remarkable when we find his pupil Scriabin combining musical art with Physical Science (see Chapter IX). He drew his examples from Palestrina, Josquin des Pres, Lassus, Willaert, Obrecht, and Morales; and his own examples are not only full of ingenuity, but, notwithstanding their mathematical correctness, possess also a distinct musical poetry. It is so easy to call him dry for this view; but his works, although all founded on the Western classical masters, reveal an originality and a musicality which should give him a high place amongst composers. His instrumentation is masterly and he made use of many new effects; he has a way of building up his choruses too in remarkable contrapuntal combinations. We find in his music many significant indications of his pupil Scriabin's orchestral style. Taneieff wrote four Symphonies but only one (Op. 12, the last), in C minor and major, is published (Belaieff, 1901). This shows him to be a profound admirer of Beethoven and a "stickler" for musical form and construction. There are two features in

[1] Leonardo da Vinci: *Libero di pittura. Parte prima*, § 1.

this Symphony which evidently impressed Scriabin, for he used them in his Second Symphony (composed shortly after it) and later on in his Third, *The Divine Poem*. One is a little quaver figure on the violins; the other, a fine suggestion of Soaring by broad, rising curves of melody on the strings. There is too in this Symphony that clever unification of the movements by derivation, which we find in Scriabin. Taneieff wrote much fine Chamber Music also. His *Ten Songs*, Op. 26 (1909) and his *Seven Songs*, Op. 30 (1912), to Russian words, it is true, do not rise to a high level; they closely resemble Weingartner's German songs. His Overture to *Orestes*, Op. 6, however, reveals a fine dramatic power. His large and very valuable library would doubtless be open to young Scriabin.[1]

Scriabin was equally fortunate in his pianoforte teacher. Safonoff's fame as a conductor is world-wide. He has always been a musician of marvellous insight and great executive gifts; an artist of great ideals and a man of large humanity and fine linguistic gifts. I remember meeting him on his first visit to England. He was entertained at a civic function, and after dinner he gave his first speech in English—an address of great power—on the Power of Music in life. It was given in faultless, flowing English with great dramatic power and eloquence. If Scriabin did not derive his own high ideals from Safonoff, he must have felt himself repeatedly confirmed and strengthened in them by

[1] Taneieff died on June 6, 1915 (New Style, June 19).

regular contact with such a man. Safonoff was the son of a Russian general, and was born in 1852 in the Northern Caucasus.[1] After finishing a Course of Jurisprudence at the Alexandrovsky Lycée, Petrograd, during which period he studied with Leschetizsky, he threw up law for music in 1826. Having studied musical theory privately under Sieke and Zaremba, he entered the Petrograd Conservatoire in 1878, studying the piano under Louis Brassin. The 'Cellist, Carl Davidoff, who was then Principal, gave him a Piano Sub-Professorship. In 1885 Tchaikovsky appointed him Chief Professor of Pianoforte Playing at the Moscow Conservatoire. He succeeded Taneieff there as Principal in 1889, but resigned in 1906 to take up a post in New York.

After some years Taneieff relinquished his tutorial work in order to devote himself entirely to composition. Scriabin was then removed to Arensky's class. Anton Stefanovitch Arensky was born at Nijni Novgorod in 1861. He died prematurely when on a holiday at Terioky in Finland. He studied first at Rousseau's Music School at Petrograd, under Zieke, and then at the age of 18, with Rimsky-Korsakoff and Johansen at the Petrograd Conservatoire. In 1882 his *Piano Concerto*, Op. 2, and his First Symphony, Op. 4, met with a great success, and in the same year he was appointed to the Moscow Conservatoire as Professor of Harmony and Counterpoint. He founded his musical style

[1] At Istchory, a picturesque village on the swiftly flowing river Terek.

very largely on Tchaikovsky and indulged very freely in 5–4 time. He was ten years the senior of Scriabin, but like many other masters of a future famous composer he does not seem to have appreciated the gifts and possibilities of young Scriabin at all. Far from encouraging, he failed to find in his brilliant pupil any justification for following the career of a composer.[1] Alexander left Arensky's class at the end of the term in disgust. Probably Arensky wanted to " put him back too far." At any rate negotiations were completely broken off. Scriabin concluded his pianoforte classes with Safonoff in 1891. But the last term at his beloved Conservatoire was by no means fruitless; for it was there he met the great patron, and publisher of music, Belaieff, and a friendship with him began then, which lasted until the publisher's death.

Mitrophan Petrovitch Belaieff was born at Petrograd in 1836. He was attracted to music from his earliest years; but it was not until he was nearly fifty years of age that he devoted himself entirely to music publishing. He died on January 4, 1904, leaving many well-endowed musical institutions and the famous "Belaieff Edition," which is devoted entirely to Russian composers. He published the whole of Scriabin's Symphonies as they were written, had Pianoforte arrangements made from the full scores, and issued no less than two-thirds of the whole of Scriabin's pianoforte compositions. He assisted Scriabin also by arranging concert-tours and in numberless other ways. Whilst

[1] Verdi suffered a similar discouragement.

VASSILY ILYITCH SAFONOFF
(CONDUCTOR OF SCRIABIN'S SYMPHONIES)

Photo by Histed]

at the Conservatoire, Scriabin had published a few pieces with Jurgenson the Moscow publisher:

Op.
1. *Waltz in F minor.*
2. (*a*) *Étude.*
   (*b*) *Prelude.*
   (*c*) *Impromptu à la Mazur.*
3. *Ten Mazurkas* (2 Books).

They probably belong to the days of the Cadet School. They are entirely Chopinesque in feeling and in style, but the left hand is already busy with Scriabinesque stretching, there is a fondness for tenor counter-melodies and a finished style of harmony and phrasing. The *Prelude*, Op. 2 (*b*), in B,[1] is a little gem—just sixteen bars in all; it is one of the most charming miniatures in the whole range of music. In the third Opus there are more evidences of originality: and the pieces are so highly finished and really artistic that it is difficult to realise that they are the work of a youth of seventeen. Already he is seeking a greater sonority, the left-hand chords reach a twelfth in width. The first piece in the second book is one of the sunniest little works in the whole of Scriabin's output. In his search for light, he goes right to the very top of the keyboard. The dreamy Chopin-like episodes are still in evidence. The spirit of Tchaikovsky creeps into the last piece of this set, in which a chiming as of a high bell is mingled with a deep tolling in the bass.

[1] This is transcribed for the Organ in my *Russian Organ Album* (Augener).

Opus 4, *Allegro Appassionata*, full of deep Brahmsian brooding, with a vigorous cross-phrased arpeggio in the bass, and Opus 5, *Two Nocturnes*, also belong to the early days at the Conservatoire, although not published till 1894 by Belaieff.

There have recently come to light three unnumbered Compositions :

Fantasia for piano and orchestra
Five-part fugue for Piano
Nocturne in A flat

belonging to the same early period. The first two were found at Professor Rozenoff's of the Moscow Conservatoire, a fellow student with Scriabin there in the early days. The *Nocturne* was discovered at L. Sabanieff's, and dates from the autumn of 1886. I hope no attempt will be made to publish them. The *Fantasia* is only in the form of a transcription for two pianos; the *Fugue* is evidently a school work, whilst the Nocturne cannot now add anything to the lustre of the composer.

With regard to the fondness of Chopin and later on of Scriabin, for the Nocturne form, it is a comforting thought to remember that an Englishman, John Field, was the inventor of it. His pieces are probably not sufficiently well known in England on account of his having spent the greater part of his life in Petrograd. But Field's personal connection with Russian music was closer even than this; for the future founder of Russian national

Opera, Glinka, was brought to him as a boy for lessons, and when Field left Petrograd for Moscow he passed young Glinka over to his favourite pupil Obmana. So that we see the Anglo-Russian musical *entente* is no new thing.

V

DEVELOPMENT: A MAN WITH AN IDEA

"A prophet is not without honour save in his own country."
Matt. xiii. 57.

SCRIABIN'S music-classes at the Conservatoire terminated in 1891. His Cadet education was completed a little earlier. And now he felt himself free to follow the career of a pianist and composer, with a strong inclination towards this latter solely. Although he received his entire schooling in the Cadet Corps, there seems to have been no question of his adopting a military career. His foster-parents seemed to have taken for granted all along that music was to be his life's work, and to have done everything to help in this direction. The old prejudice against a musical life which was such a barrier to the older Russian composers had now passed away. Tchaikovsky was thwarted in every way in adopting music until he was thirty years old, and that fine musical genius Cesar Cui all through his life followed the dual profession of music and military engineering. Cui was a great authority on fortifications, and numbered amongst his pupils, the present Czar and General Skobeleff. . . . Then, too, the growing acceptance of Russian music in France and the Netherlands, in England and America impressed the Russian *intelligentsia* very much. In Brussels and Paris the Countess Mercy Argenteau carried on a strenuous campaign on its behalf.

But it was the meeting with the fine-spirited publisher Belaieff which formed the real opening-out point in Scriabin's career. Belaieff had immediately recognised the fine genius of the young musician, and constituted himself his sole publisher under a favourable pecuniary arrangement which placed Scriabin in a fairly easy position right up to the time of Belaieff's death in 1892. Belaieff's first step was to organise a European tour for the young pianist. This included Amsterdam, Brussels, the Hague, Paris, and Berlin. The twenty-year-old composer, who appeared only in his own compositions on this tour, was received favourably everywhere. The pieces which he played were the *First Sonata*, Op. 6, the *Allegro Appassionata*, Op. 4, and a few smaller pieces. On his return to Russia he played his own works at concerts in Moscow, Petrograd, and many other cities.

The following five years—1893 to 1897—were occupied in concert tours, holiday-travels, and composition. The last two seemed to have been always connected in his work, for he drew his inspiration from Nature more perhaps than any other musician since the time of Beethoven and Brahms. His highly sensitive and impressionable mind responded easily to the appeal of Nature, especially in her summer garb ; and his very first orchestral composition—a *Reverie* for Orchestra in E

—is evidently a summer meditation in the country. He was very responsive to this mood, and twice reproduced it again later on in important compositions—in his *First Symphony* (2nd movement) and in his *Second* (3rd movement).

The young Russian does not incline much to sports and athletics, and has few hobbies, other than indoor amusements. With Scriabin, it was chess in the winter. For the rest, music seems to have been his sole hobby and the most engrossing thing in life. I do not think that he was ever a great reader, except of that greatest book of all—NATURE herself. He was passionately fond of the country, of flowers, and of travelling. His favourite costume in the summer was an English-looking lounge suit, a large flowing art tie, a broad-spreading panama hat, and—button shoes. The prevailing note of the costume was a refined ease. And the creations of these five easy years were :

Op.
6. **First Sonata.**
7. *Two Impromptus.*
8. *Twelve Études.*
9. *Prelude and Nocturne* (*for left hand only*).
10. *Two Impromptus.*
11. *Twenty-four Preludes.*
12. *Two Impromptus.*
13. *Six Preludes.*
14. *Two Impromptus.*
15. *Five Preludes.*
16. *Five Preludes.*
17. *Seven Preludes.*

Op.
18. *Allegro de Concert.*
19. **Second Sonata.**
20. **Pianoforte Concerto.**
21. *Polonaise in B flat minor.*
22. *Four Preludes.*
24. **Third Sonata.**
25. *Nine Mazurkas.*
26. **First Symphony.**

This is a pretty good list—five large works and some eighty smaller ones. The FIRST SYMPHONY (E major) was produced at one of the Belaieff Russian Symphony Concerts given by the I.R.M.O. (*Imperatorskoe Russisky Musikalne Obstchestivo*—the Imperial Russian Musical Society), under the baton of Safonoff, Principal of the Conservatoire. This Symphony is in six movements—a meditative *Lento*, an *Allegro dramatico* with some fine "string" work, a *Vivace* in 9-8, an *Allegro* in E minor, and a Choral Epilogue and Fugue "In Praise of Art." Although so early a production, with shadows of Dvorak and Tchaikovsky passing over it, it is nevertheless a masterly work of great beauty. The basses have frequent melodies of great beauty, but the Choral Fugue smells too much of the Academy.

The work was well received. Strange to say Arensky disliked it, and once, whilst arguing about Scriabin, exclaimed that it was quite evident that "anyone who praised this Symphony knew nothing at all about music." Such an attitude is incomprehensible. But it was only the beginning of a slowly built up and formidable opposition to Scriabin in Moscow, an opposition which lasted more or less right up to his death. Did Arensky resent the precocity of this young composer who dared to begin where Beethoven had left off—with a Choral Symphony? Or was there something of progressiveness and impatience for authority and routine in Scriabin's nature which aggravated the more conservative minds? Quite probably.

Safonoff says that Scriabin, in his youth at any rate, was a man of extremes. Once just before they had parted for the holidays he had told him that his pianoforte "touch" was equal to all ethereal and tender effects, but that it wanted *deepening*. When, after the vacation, Scriabin came back to the Conservatoire, and struck a few chords on the pianoforte, it was like "two orchestras backed by a thunderstorm." . . . "Good heavens, my dear boy, what have you been doing?" Safonoff exclaimed. "Well, you told me to deepen my touch," Scriabin answered, rather aggrieved. . . . But by blending these extremes, Scriabin became at maturity one of the most perfectly equipped pianists ever heard. He could do anything with his instrument, and his pedalisation was something of a miracle.

In 1897 he was offered the post of Professor of Piano Playing at his *alma mater*—and accepted. It was a mistake. There is in the artistic nature—whether of a creative or an interpretive cast of mind—as a rule, a distinct aversion to pedagogic duties. Doubtless Scriabin felt a little proper pride in following such men as Nicolas Rubinstein (the founder), Zverieff, Arensky, and Safonoff. Perhaps too as a "free lance" he missed the Academic support of his compositions and his public appearances. Or it may have been even more practical considerations which led him to this step; for about this time he married a young and brilliant Russian pianist; and everyone knows that matrimony brings one more closely into touch with practical considerations. Be that as it may, these six years of tutorial work at the Conservatoire were "very lean years" in musical compositions. The only works dating from this period are:

Op.
27. *Two Preludes.*
28. *Fantasia in B minor.*
29. *Second Symphony.*

The marriage, too, did not prove ideal; and was dissolved later—probably by mutual consent. Marriage is a great lottery, and those happily mated are the most ready to let their sympathy flow out to those less fortunate.

The *Second Sonata* was begun in 1892, but the 2nd (final) movement was not finished until later on. The *Pianoforte Concerto* is one of his most popular works, whilst his *Third Sonata* is now a piano classic. The SECOND SYMPHONY was first produced in Moscow by the I.R.M.O. orchestra, under the expressive hands of Safonoff. It seems strange to look back now and find that even at that early stage, Scriabin was regarded as a dangerous revolutionary in music. The Symphony is in five movements, the first (*Andante*) supplying the material for the fifth (*Maestoso*, an Epilogue in C major). The three middle ones are an *Allegro*, an *Andante* (really *Adagio*), and a *Tempestuoso* which runs into the Epilogue. The orchestra, a very moderate one, is deftly handled, and there is a homogeneity in handling the themes as well as in their conception. Moreover, as in all Scriabin's works, the subjects themselves are very striking. Particularly noticeable are the beautiful singing bass parts.

Yet at the orchestral rehearsals, the players were strongly biassed against the work, some almost to the point of refusing to play in it. But this was nothing to the opposition of a certain *clique* at the Concert who disturbed the performance by howls of derision, whistling, and cat-calls. It was but the experience of Monteverde, Gluck, Handel, Beethoven and Wagner over again.[1]

Incredible as it may seem now, the Second Symphony of Scriabin appeared to them so unusual and so "ultra-modern" that it brought forth an outburst of indignation from the audience. And now this work is in the classic repertoire of all our Symphony Concerts. Even the smaller piano compositions of this period were received with perplexity when they were first played at the Kerzensky Circle.

[1] I myself once hooted Stravinsky's *Rite of Springtime*; and now, looking coolly back, I am inclined to think my resentment was based on my outraged pride at not being able to understand the work fully.

From this time there began at Moscow a " dead-set " against the composer, and all through his life he underwent in his native city a strenuous persecution on the part of his more active opponents, and a cool indifference on the part of others. Academic people regarded Scriabin with nervousness. " What will he do next ? " they seem to have been continually thinking. At Moscow, the professionals ranged themselves against him, and the public, not able to understand his works, either followed their lead, or ignored him altogether.

But Scriabin was not without enthusiastic friends. All his life he had the faculty of drawing round him keen appreciators and supporters: Belaieff, Kussevitsky, Safonoff, Gunst, Conus, Sabaneieff—these make a goodly list which was continually being increased.

All the early orchestral works of Scriabin—the *Reverie*, the *Concerto*, the *First* and *Second Symphonies*, and the *Poem of Ecstasy*—were first produced by Safonoff. In 1889 this conductor inaugurated a series of popular Concerts at moderate prices in a disused circus in Moscow. In 1890 he was appointed conductor of the Moscow branch of the I.R.M.O. He occupied this post for sixteen years, leaving the Moscow Orchestra and the Principalship of the Conservatoire in 1906 to take up the post of permanent Conductor of the New York Philharmonic Society. His renderings are characterised by great lucidity, intellectual grasp, and a full-blooded warmth, and he has specialised on Tchaikovsky's and Scriabin's orchestral works,

As time went on Scriabin found his pedagogic duties seriously clogging his creative work, and early in 1903, after six years of tutorial work at the Conservatoire, he followed Taneieff's lead and resigned his post in order to devote himself entirely to musical composition. This year proved to be one of the most fertile periods of Scriabin's life. In the summer alone he finished his *Third Symphony* (*The Divine Poem*), and wrote his *Fourth Sonata*, his *Tragedy*, and his *Poème Satanique*, and some forty other pieces. All these belong to his middle style—the transition period.

The greater part of 1904 was spent in Beattenberg, a delightful spot near Geneva. In the winter Scriabin went to Paris, where his *Divine Poem* (*Third Symphony*) was brought to a first hearing under Arthur Nikisch[1] on May 29, 1905 (N.S.). The Symphony, thus first produced abroad, was later on well received in Moscow, to which city the composer did not return, however, for seven years.

The nomenclature of the Third Symphony (*The Divine Poem*), with its three movements headed *Luttes* (Strife), *Voluptes* (Sensuous Joys), and *Jeu divin* (Divine Activity), calls for some remark; and

[1] Arthur Nikisch was born in Hungary in 1855. He studied at the Vienna Conservatoire with the violin as his principal study. He afterwards received appointments as conductor at various Austrian and German cities. In 1889 he took up the conductorship of the Boston Symphony Orchestra, remaining there for four years, when he returned as Director of the Buda-Pesth Opera House. In 1906 he held the posts of conductor of Leipzig Gewandhaus Concerts and of the Berlin Philharmonic Society. He has travelled widely as a "star-conductor."

it is just at this juncture that so little first-hand information is forthcoming.

Scriabin left Moscow in 1903, and with the exception of long periodic returns to Beattenberg in Switzerland, and a two years' sojourn in Brussels, was a bird of passage and a holiday wanderer for many years. Being of a very reserved nature, he became, as years went on, more and more detached, isolated, and self-centred in his music. He toured widely, visiting all the chief European cities from time to time, and travelling where his fancy led him; but in general, like Brahms, he loved most to live in beautiful climes and to spend much of his time in self-communion and meditation.

Since the religious enfranchisement in Russia many new cults have arisen there. Amongst these, Theosophy has been much favoured amongst the *intelligentsia*, especially in Moscow and Charkoff. People seem to be experiencing a desire for a greater spirituality than is afforded by the older forms. Scriabin's music appears to have joined issue with Theosophy as a convenient peg to hang his music on. The peg has very little concern with the garment which hangs on it, and I am inclined to think it is so with Scriabin's Theosophy and his music. Of course I am not doubting for one moment Scriabin's single-mindedness in this practice, for sincerity was one of the dominant notes of his character. Most composers at some time or other feel the need of some system of æsthetics or some explanation (even tabulation) of those special moods which return upon them from time to time and are reflected in their music—the contemplation mood, the exalted one, the pastoral vein, the exhilaration of life, and so on. We are told that Scriabin's Theosophy grew out of his music. I can imagine rather that when Scriabin encountered Theosophy he immediately embraced a system which harmonised so well with his prevailing musical moods. I do not think, however, we ought to judge Theosophy by his music; or his music by Theosophy. We shall discuss this matter further in a later chapter.

This THIRD SYMPHONY is a magnificent composition, written on the soundest of classical lines, on a musical architecture approximating closely to that of César Franck in his Quintet, his Quartet, and other works. That is, it has a Prologue which contains the basic idea of the work, and which runs through all the other movements in addition to and in connection with their usual theme. Scriabin regards this leading motive as his Divine Theme, and most of the other subjects are derived from it. There is no doubt that the unusual labelling of his movements in his Symphonies perplexed many people, and consequently often aroused ire. But the movements of this Symphony by any other names would sound as sweet; indeed, after reading the unusual titles, I confess on the first hearing to a little disappointment at the absolute orthodoxy of the music. But I did not know then that, titles or no titles, Scriabin is the real composer of Absolute Music (as opposed to Programme Music) and a Classicist at heart.

The Symphony, with its noble themes and its brilliant orchestration, had a great success at Paris—that city which has always been drawn so enthusiastically to Russian music. Tchaikovsky was well known and loved by them fifteen years before we became acquainted with him in England or America.

Scriabin spent the winter 1905–6 in a villa on the outskirts of Genoa. He left it in February for Geneva, where he lived until December 2. He then embarked on a tour in the United States, playing in New York, Chicago, Washington, Cincinnati, Detroit, and other cities with great success.

Shortly after his return to Paris his *Second Symphony* and his *Pianoforte Concerto* were given at Diagelieff's[1] Symphony Concerts there, the solo part in the Concerto being played by Mr. Josef Hoffman. This famous pianist was born at Cracow in 1877. His father was the chief conductor at the Warsaw Opera House and a Professor at the Warsaw Conservatoire. Josef studied under his father for several years, and finally with Rubinstein (1892–4), after which he made a world tour as a juvenile prodigy. He was wisely withdrawn from the platform for several years, and has now developed into one of the finest exponents of modern piano playing, with a special turn for the orchestral

[1] Diagelieff is a Russian conductor who made world tours with a Russian Opera and Ballet troupe, and who also frequently conducted concerts of Russian orchestral music in various large cities in Europe and America.

development of pianoforte tone. He is a special favourite in Paris as in Moscow, and has always been an enthusiastic propagator and exponent of Scriabin's music.

Scriabin spent the summer of 1907 at Beattenberg on the lovely shores of Geneva. The works which date from this period are—

Op.
44. *Two Poems.*
45. *Three Morceaux.*
46. *Scherzo.*
47. *Quasi-Valse.*
48. *Four Preludes.*
49. *Three Morceaux* (*Étude, Prelude, Reverie*).
51. *Four Pieces.*
52. *Three Pieces.*

They are all of exquisite beauty; and although founded on the older harmonic lines, have ample evidence of a distinct advance on any of the preceding great composers. Opus 50 is not forthcoming; perhaps it was lost.

He spent the winter at his father's house in Lausanne. The Ex-Consul of Erzeroum had retired to this lovely spot some years before. There the composer finished his orchestral piece, *The Poem of Ecstasy*, in January, 1908. No sooner was this completed than he set to and wrote the *Fifth Piano Sonata*—in the incredibly short space of three or four days. These two remarkable works are closely related in conception and in style. Together they represent perhaps better than any other the boundary line between his older style and his new. The summer of 1908 was spent at Biarritz, and in September he went to Brussels, in which city he domiciled for two years. There his masterpiece *Prometheus* was conceived and the greater part of it written.

Although I can find little exact information about the circumstances which drew him and held him in this beautiful city, yet it is reasonable to infer that a special sympathy, not to say influence, was instrumental in his choice of this brilliant capital for a residence. At that time Brussels, more than any other European city (not even excepting Paris), had some exceptionally brilliant coteries of artists, thinkers, and musicians—men whose minds were seriously drawn to a possible close connection between the Sciences and the Arts, and even Philosophy and Religion.

The brilliant Jean Delville had just brought out, in 1900, his study and meditation on *The Mission of Art*. This series of essays impatiently throwing aside the old shackles which impeded conventional art was yet at the opposite pole to the crude, barbarous works of the French Fauvists, Cubists, and the like, to the German Realists or the noisy Florentine Academy. It was Delville, one of the leaders of this Theosophist cult in Brussels, who drew the design for the cover of Scriabin's *Prometheus* copies.

In the preface to Delville's book, Edward Schure writes: " See here the book of a true young man; the act of a thinker, of an artist, and of a seer, a witness to science, enthusiasm, and faith." We find Delville writing thus: "It is wise to meditate frequently in an epoch such as ours where the most unshapely works pass as arch-types of the so-called 'free' styles. Art and literature have lost the sense of the divine. One knows only too well the artistic decadence brought about through the negligence or the poverty of these artists without design; and if ugliness has replaced beauty in art nowadays, it is because art has lost the abstract and vital sense of Form. The Line, is it not the basis of all architecture, of all statuary? The Line in all the objects of Nature that is the Signature of God" (p. 47).

One cannot read this without remembering Scriabin's absolute mastery and reverence for form and clearness of construction in music. More than any other master, he uses the clean-cut four-bar phrase, almost invariably in fact. Nor can we fail to notice the influence of the great Belgian poets, Maeterlinck, and also of Verhaeren, one of the editors of *L'Art Moderne*, whose poems seem to have so close an affinity to the later Sonatas of Scriabin.

The Brussels of 1908 was indeed brilliantly represented in Science, Art, and Philosophy, and certainly no less in Music. The Opera-house apart—itself one of the best equipped and most modern in Europe—there was an unusually large number of brilliant artistes: Eugene Ysaye, the great violinist; Paul Gilson, the illustrious composer of the opera *Francesca da Rimini* and author of one of the finest works on the modern orchestra; that refined musical theorist, Emile d'Ergo, whose *Dans les Propylées de l'instrumentation* is a wonder-work; those brilliant experimenters, Robert Mahrhofer, author of *The Psychology of Tone-Colours*, F. A. Gevaert, part author of *The Musical Problem of Aristotle;* and many other keen musical philosophers in acoustics and especially in orchestral tone-colour. One of the Professors at the Conservatoire there illustrated a lecture of his by having the whole of the intact score of a Mozartean Symphony played solely by instruments of the clarinet family. Moreover, there were here in Brussels some of the most superb orchestras in the world; and the Brussellaise, always the most generous of people, opened their arms freely to artists and composers from all quarters. Even a little of the best English music arrived there, though unknown in France, Germany, or Russia.[1] Moreover, Brussels has always led the van in its timely welcome of Russian music. Enough has been said to explain the attraction which this eminently artistic city exerted over Scriabin. He abode there two years, and he there met his second wife.

The actual compositions of his sojourn in Brussels are not great in number; but the inclusion of his great tone-poem *Prometheus* makes up the sum-total in bulk and importance; and the other

[1] Emil Cooper (the Russianised English Conductor), however, has recently given Elgar's *Falstaff* and Wallace's *Villon* in Moscow.

pieces constitute some of his most characteristic works :

Op.
56. *Four Pieces* (*Prelude, Ironies, Nuances, Étude*).
57. *Two Pieces* (*Desir, Caresse dansée*).
58. *Feuillet d'Album* (*for the New Russian Album*).
59. *Two Pieces* (*Poem, Prelude*).
60. "*Prometheus*" (*Orchestral Poem*).

It was in 1909 that he paid a flying visit from his Brussels home to Moscow to take part in a concert arranged there in his honour. The Russian Imperial Musical Society gave his *Third Symphony* (*The Divine Poem*) at one of their Symphony Concerts, and also the new *Poem of Ecstasy*, the latter for the first time in public. Safonoff was the conductor, and Scriabin played his own *Fifth Sonata*.

He made an entirely successful appearance on this occasion, which was, however, slightly discounted by a hostile attack from the chief music-critic of the *Russkoye Slovo* (*Russian Word*), a leading Moscow "daily," who rained abuse on Scriabin's mystic titles, even likening them to "beer-bottle labels." When this attack fell to the ground harmlessly, he accused the author of *L'Ecstasy* of deliberately, ignoring "all that nationally Russian undying art created by Glinka, Borodin, and Rimsky-Korsakoff," and described Scriabin's music as "the outcome of all that was worst in Wagner and Strauss." In other words, Scriabin was "a

Germanophile in the worst sense of the term and a wilful scorner of Russian culture." All this of course was very childish, and moreover it was not "criticism." A young reviewer on the same paper wrote glowing accounts of Scriabin's works, especially with regard to the piano pieces which Scriabin rendered at the concerts in Sokolnikoff.

There were other mementoes of this visit to his native city, however, which served to mitigate the *Russian Word* critic's spiteful attack. One was the bestowal of a "Glinka prize" on the *Poem of Ecstasy*. Some years before, Belaieff, the music publisher, had founded an endowed Annual Award "In Memory of Glinka" for the encouragement of Russian musical composers. In December of this year (1908) the awards were particularly interesting:

1st Prize (1000 roubles). Sergiùs Rachmaninoff for his *Symphony*.
2nd Prize (700 roubles). Alexander Scriabin for *Poem of Ecstasy*.
3rd Prize (500 roubles). Alexander Spendiaroff for *The Three Palm Trees*.
4th Prize (500 roubles). Sergius Taneieff for his *Pianoforte Trio*.

Sergius Vassilivitch Rachmaninoff (of C sharp minor Prelude fame) was a fellow-student with Scriabin at the Moscow Conservatoire. He was born in the government of Nijni Novgorod in 1873, and studied at Moscow with Zviereff, Siloti (his kinsman), Taneieff, and Arensky. His style is somewhat conventional, and obviously founded largely on Taneieff's and Arensky's, but he has great musical gifts, ease in composition, and a clearness of musical diction which renders his music very taking and popular. His *Symphony* is a long work on classical lines, more than twice the duration of Scriabin's *L'Ecstasy,* which plays for twenty minutes or so. Spendiaroff's piece was an orchestral tone-poem of an Oriental character, based on a poem of Pushkin. It was first performed in Moscow in December of the preceding year (1907) under the baton of Glazounoff.

Taneieff was the tutor of all the other three prize winners. He excels in chamber music. His style, however, is very scholastic and intellectual in type. His Trio was first performed in January, 1908.

. . . . . .

Doubtless the followers of Rachmaninoff's somewhat facile art could hardly be keen appreciators of Scriabin's music; but despite a certain hostile camp, Scriabin was becoming more and more firmly established as a composer in his native land. His performances in Russia were always successful and well received on the part of the public.

. . . . . .

Scriabin returned to Brussels, and settled down again to work at his great orchestral work *Prometheus,* which he did not actually complete till the following year, when the Scriabins left Brussels and settled in Moscow in the quiet little Tolstovsky

Street. Scriabin was heartily welcomed by his friend Kussevitzsky, the famous conductor; and many of the younger professors at the Conservatoire rallied round him, notably the pianists: Eugen Gunst, an enthusiastic advocate of Scriabin, and Léon Sabaneieff and Léon Conus, son of the old professor. Kussevitzsky invited Scriabin to accompany him on his first Volga tour (1910), an offer which the composer accepted gladly.

Sergius Alexandrovitch Kussevitzsky is one of the most prominent figures in Russian musical life. Born and educated in Russia, a student at the Moscow Conservatoire, he travelled widely, but finally settled down with Moscow as a centre. He began his career as a double-bass player, having a remarkable technique and a peculiarly poetic tone. Later on he was drawn to conducting, and organised Symphony Concerts, founding his own orchestra (with a chorus for use in symphonic works) in 1911. His Moscow Symphony Concerts are repeated a week later in Petrograd, Kussevitzsky taking his whole orchestra with him. He has performed a very special work for Russian music by establishing a special music publishing business in Moscow,[1] with branches at Petrograd and Berlin. This affords Russian composers a particularly generous profit for their works. He was the first in Russia to organise musical festivals devoted to a single composer: to Bach, to Beethoven, and to Tchaikovsky. In 1910 he commenced the vast undertaking of taking his whole orchestra up and down the Volga

[1] Russian Music Publishing Society. See p. 278.

on a specially chartered steamboat, playing the great musical masterpieces at the various cities *en route*—at Novgorod, Charkoff, Saratoff, Odessa, and other cities. On this first Volga tour, Scriabin played his early *Piano Concerto* and other pieces of his own music.

VI

CODA: THE LAST YEARS

SCRIABIN returned to Moscow very pleased with the Kussevitzsky Volga tour (1910). But he returned to a Moscow groaning under a stifling heat. In summer the city becomes intolerable with the glare of the sun, the noises of vehicles over the cobbled streets, and the odious smells inseparable *apparently* from manufacture in large cities. Scriabin, following his usual custom, retreated to the country, this time to the Mark estate in the Savelovsky Railway. He did not return to Moscow till the winter. On March 2, 1911, *Prometheus : the Poem of Fire* was brought to a first hearing. This was given at one of Kussevitzsky's Symphony Concerts at Moscow, and Scriabin himself took the pianoforte part in it. One was not surprised to read in the Russian papers that opinions were much divided over this extremely advanced work. The spring of 1911 was spent at his most favoured retreat—Beattenberg, on Lake Geneva. Here he finished his *Sixth* and *Seventh Sonatas* and made sketches for another, which appears later on as the Ninth. Why such beautiful surroundings should inspire such gloomy works as the *Sixth* and *Seventh Sonatas* perhaps only a Theosophist can tell. A visit to

Brussels followed, and after a six weeks' sojourn in this city, he toured through Holland with the conductor Mengelburg, who produced many of Scriabin's orchestral works, the new *Prometheus* figuring on every programme. The tour, which included Amsterdam, the Hague, Haarlem, and even extended to Frankfurt-on-Maine, was one long triumph for Scriabin. He returned to Russia and spent the late summer and autumn on the Obrazchovo-Karpovo estate near the town of Kaskir. He made an extensive Russian tour in the winter season 1911–12, and in April, 1912, took a house in the Great Nikolai Peskovsky Street in Arbatte, a suburb of Moscow. Here he composed his later pianoforte works :

Op.
65. *Three Études ;*
66. *Eighth Sonata ;*
67. *Two Preludes ;*
69. *Two Poems ;*
70. *Tenth Sonata ;*

and finished the *Ninth Sonata,* which he had sketched out in Switzerland in the preceding year.

At the beginning of 1914 he visited London for the first time, and was much impressed by the English people. On March 14 his *Prometheus* was produced at the Queen's Hall, under Sir Henry Wood. He also played in his *Pianoforte Concerto* on that occasion. The *Prometheus* had been given in London the previous year, on which occasion (January 2, 1913) it was played twice over by

ALEXANDER SCRIABIN

(1911)

special request, with the idea that a second hearing would make the work more easily intelligible.

The Queen's Hall Programme on this occasion was:

1. *Symphony No. 8* (*Beethoven*).
2. *Piano Concerto in F sharp minor*, Op. 20 (*Scriabin*).
3. *Tone Poem "Prometheus,"* Op. 60 (*Scriabin*).
4. *Tone Poem "Tod und Verklärung"* (*Strauss*).
5. *Overture "Meistersinger"* (*Wagner*).

Although Scriabin's appearance in his two works was a great success, it cannot be said that his *Prometheus* was widely understood, and the advanced modernity of the work brought forth, even in enlightened London, a few vigorous marks of disapproval. The London season was an exceptionally full one that year, and it was characterised by an almost wild straining after the new at all costs in the arts, painting, literature, and music. The critics, already sated with the modernity of Mahler, the ultra-modernity of Schönberg, and the freaks of the Cubists, were inclined to place Scriabin with the general mass of the "unintelligibles," and either condemned the work whole-heartedly or else confessed themselves mystified. I have expressed elsewhere the opinion that the works should be heard in historical order. The gradual and wonderful evolution through which Scriabin's creations passed between his early *Concerto*, Op. 20, and his most advanced work *Prometheus*, explains and accounts for everything. It is necessary that the intervening works should be heard; or at least something read about them.

A. N. Briantchaninoff, a Russian critic, who was present at the Queen's Hall Concert, considers that the audience could not grasp the intention and inner meaning of *Prometheus,* which is "too far not only from Beethoven but also from Wagner." Though he himself has heard the tone-poem five times, there are still parts of it which he cannot endure, and he thinks that the audience shared his feelings of "infinite amazement, extreme nervous tension, and boundless enthusiasm for the ray of sunshine with which, at the very end, Scriabin pierces the gloomy mist of that undoubted work of genius."

In spite of the ovation which Scriabin received (and music-lovers who have attended London concerts for thirty years do not remember such an ovation) it must be recognised, says Briantchaninoff, that the performance, "notwithstanding all the careful rehearsal, left much to be desired. There was no feeling of that subtle mysticism with which every phrase should be filled, in preparation for the apotheosis of the final theme. It was a conscientious, even a fine musical performance. But that is all!"

"*Prometheus* is far more than the ordinary tone-poem, and its inner meaning can only be deciphered by those who understand the composer's mystical temperament. Sir Henry Wood and his orchestra were not of that number, and therefore there was no 'inward fire' in the rendering of the *Poem of Fire*." "From a purely musical point of view the *Finale*, which usually produces such an overwhelming effect, was imperfect; the bells were weak and there was no chorus at all. Those who heard *Prometheus* in Amsterdam last year, under Mendelberg, when a chorus of five hundred took part in the *Finale*, will know how much the London performance lost in this respect. In justice to Wood, it should be stated that there appear to be no good choruses in London, and to get one together from the provinces for a single performance would cost over 2000 roubles, which is more than even the Queen's Hall could stand.[1] But, after such a memorable success, it is impossible to doubt that for the next season all the arrangements will be perfect. Scriabin has conquered London. It is difficult to overcome the English, but once they yield they do so entirely, unconditionally, and there are no more steadfast enthusiasms than those of the English."

Even the two beautiful Piano Recitals which Scriabin gave at the Bechstein Hall, although immensely appreciated by crowded audiences, did not make the deep impression they would certainly have done in a more normal season. Here are the Programmes. The E flat *Étude*, Op. 11, No. 14 appears on both Programmes. So too do the second and last numbers of Opus 8. Even so advanced a piece as *Étrangeté* was encored.

[1] It is amusing to see ourselves as others see us.

BECHSTEIN HALL

MARCH 20TH, 1914

PROGRAMME

I

PRÉLUDES . .	C major, Op. 13.	
	G sharp minor E minor C major C sharp minor E sharp minor E flat minor D major D minor	Op. 11.
MAZURKAS . .	E flat minor F sharp major	Op. 3.
ÉTUDES . . .	F sharp minor A flat major D sharp minor	Op. 8.

II

3ME SONATE . . F sharp minor, Op. 23.

(*a*) *Allegro dramatico.*
(*b*) *Allegretto.*
(*c*) *Andante.*
(*d*) *Presto.*

III

POÈME . . .	F sharp major, No. 1, Op. 32.
POÈME AILÉ . .	No. 3, Op. 51.
DÉSIR . . .	Op. 57.
ÉTRANGETÉ . .	Op. 63.
FEUILLET D'ALBUM .	Op. 59.
POÈME SATANIQUE .	Op. 36.

BECHSTEIN HALL

MARCH 26TH, 1914

PROGRAMME

I

PRÉLUDES . .	B flat major, D flat major — Op. 35.
	D minor, C minor — Op. 17.
	E flat minor, Op. 11.
	B major, G sharp minor, G flat major, E flat minor, F sharp major — Op. 16.
MAZURKAS . .	F minor, E minor — Op. 25.
ÉTUDES . .	F sharp minor, C sharp minor, D sharp minor — Op. 8.

II

SONATE FANTAISIE . No. 2, Op. 19.
(*a*) *Andante.*
(*b*) *Presto.*

III

DEUX POÈMES .	F sharp major, D major — Op. 32.
POÈME . . .	No. 1, Op. 69.
MASQUE . . .	Op. 63.
PRÉLUDE . .	No. 1, Op. 67.
POÈME . . .	No. 2, Op. 69.
SONATE . . .	No. 9, Op. 68.

Everyone was struck by what appeared to be almost a new kind of Pianism. His playing was so easy, so refined, quiet, and unassuming, yet so beautifully ethereal in the softest passages, so rich and organ-like in the *mezzo* parts, yet so satisfying in the *fortissimi*, and his "pedal" effects were quite magical in effect. It appeared as though this new music had brought along with it a new kind of playing. And so it has!

All were unanimous in agreeing that his works had become much clearer under the composer's own interpretation, and Scriabin returned home to Moscow justifiably pleased with his London success, and furnished with invitations to revisit England in the following season 1914–15, having been engaged to play at twelve concerts. . . . This second visit, alas, never took place. The European War broke out, and the London appearance in his *Prometheus* proved to be the composer's last visit abroad.

Scriabin thought he had returned to an enlightened Moscow, for during his eight years' sojourn abroad much had taken place in Russian science, art, and general enlightenment. Many progressive movements too had been opened up. A Modern Art Theatre had been founded in Moscow, the staging of which Gordon Craig considered to be second to none. Kommisarzhevskaia, the great actress, had experimented widely and liberally, and although she felt finally that her own peculiar art of acting was suffering in the process, still her influence on the Russian public has been immense. The

French Impressionists too had made a definite mark on both Russian painting and music. But the old enmities arose afresh against Scriabin. The chief Reviewer of the *Russian Word* returned to his attacks on this great artist of such exquisite sensitiveness. Criticism with this reviewer was degraded to personal abuse, to long strings of epithets poured on the man who dared to think that art should ever advance beyond the canons on which the critic himself had been brought up—and as for a new art-language, or a revived sense of hearing—to his mind anyone who ever asserted this, much less practised it—was consequently a charlatan and an impostor. . . . Good heavens! why? Only a press-man can say. . . . It is always so.

. . . . . .

This summer of 1914 was spent in Moscow, where his *Prometheus* was down for its second performance in Moscow—this time by the Orchestra of the Imperial Russian Musical Society under Safonoff. But a very definite opposition was led by the critic already alluded to, who was one of the directors of these Symphony Concerts; and his policy was carried—a policy which included the withdrawal of *Prometheus*, leaving only the early *Concerto* to represent Scriabin. The composer, who was to have appeared in both works at this Concert, withdrew altogether. Scriabin was only experiencing the intrigues which have always beset great men—from Gluck, Mozart, Beethoven onwards. Mere "nobodies" are set up against them in ridiculous competition, and too frequently the "nobodies" win—*for a time.* And then the nobodies disappear —or are only remembered with scorn.

Scriabin's almost super-sensitive nature must have felt this Moscow opposition keenly all through his career, for he loved his native city dearly; he had many friends there, and despite all the opposition of the "routine followers" he had an ever-growing public of keen appreciators. The last ten pianoforte pieces:

Op.
71. *Deux Poèmes*
72. *Vers la flamme* (*Poème*)
73. (i) *Guirlandes;* (ii) *Flammes sombres*
74. *Cinq Préludes*

were written in the spring of 1914, a year before his death; and in Op. 74, some of the harsh clashes of the materialistic world with the higher thoughts are painfully reflected. In the summer Scriabin gave himself up entirely to the realisation of his long-cherished project, the composition of a great art-work entitled *Mystery.* This was to be a creation involving the unification of all the arts in the service of one perfect religious Rite. The secondary arts were to enhance the dominating arts (those subject to the will-power). Symphonies of music, words, and *mimique* (gesture) were to be accompanied by symphonies of colour and perfume. Such a union already exists to some extent in religious rituals. With Scriabin the onlookers and listeners (the passively initiated) were also to participate in the manifestation of the creative spirit, just as much as the celebrants (or executants) of the Rite. In this proposed union of the arts, Scriabin's aim was to have been the production of an ecstatic state, affording a glimpse of higher spiritual planes. He wrote the first libretto for the Prologue[1] in the summer, which was spent in the country near Podolsky. Scriabin then set to work on the music for this Introduction and looked forward to its completion by the Spring. . . . In the winter season, 1914, Kussevitzsky gave the *Divine Poem* (*Third Symphony*) and the *Poem of Ecstasy*, and Scriabin himself gave several Piano Recitals of his own compositions to enthusiastic audiences.

In August the great European War broke out. Austria declared war on Servia, Russia on Austria, Germany on Russia, France on Germany, and within a few weeks, Belgium had been grossly trodden under foot, and England had joined against the Central Powers. The Russians twice went forward and backward over unfortunate Poland, and Moscow became one great war depot. The whole aspect of the city was changed. All the eligible men were away at the front. Trains full of soldiers left Moscow day and night. The street tramcars were used for the wounded, and long strings of German prisoners were constantly being brought through on their way to the mines in Siberia.

Scriabin was not one of those who regarded the

[1] This was, however, entirely re-written by him in the following winter.

war as an unmixed evil, but he likened it to the keen wind of Nature blowing through the world that those things which can be shaken—like materialism, intellectualism, and positivism—shall be shaken, and things which cannot be shaken—like religion, love, and truth—shall remain. He expressed the view that the terrible troubles brought by the war would bring new life, new ideas, and a finer sensibility to the nations.

In this he was singularly in accord with that fond lover of Russia, Mr. Stephen Graham, who writes thus in a recent book *Russia and the World* (Cassell) :

> "Away in the depths of man, and from deeper depths, proceeds the Almighty Voice, in whose fulfilment lies the destiny of Man and the destinies of men, and those who live in Communion know that the war is no calamity—no axe at the root, but the great storm wind of Autumn, which has blown, and will blow again, scattering the leaves and branches into the Death Kingdoms, bringing after it tears of rain, and sleep and peace, and life again—*new life.*"

In a letter addressed by Scriabin to A. N. Briantchaninoff, and published in the Moscow musical journal, *Mouzika*, he writes :

> "I cannot refrain from expressing my sympathy with the views which you have expounded

in the *Novoye Zveno* on the subject of the educational significance of war.

" You have voiced an old idea of mine, that at certain times the masses urgently need to be shaken up, in order to purify the human organisation and fit it for the reception of more delicate vibrations than those to which it has hitherto responded.

" The history of races is the expression at the periphery of the development of a central idea, which comes to the meditating prophet and is felt by the creative artist, but is completely hidden from the masses.

" The development of this idea is dependent upon the rhythm of the individual attainments, and the periodic accumulation of creative energy, acting at the periphery, produces the upheavals whereby the evolutionary movement of races is accomplished. These upheavals (cataclysms, catastrophes, wars, revolutions, etc.), in shaking the souls of men, open them to the reception of the idea hidden behind the outward happenings.

" The circle is complete, and a stage of the journey is finished: something has been attained, the creative idea has made one more impression on matter. We are now living through just such a period of upheaval, and in my eyes it is an indication that once again an idea has matured and is eager to be incarnated.

" And at such a time one wants to cry aloud to all who are capable of new conceptions, scientists, and artists, who have hitherto held aloof from the common life, but who, in fact, are unconsciously creating history. The time has come to summon them to the construction of new forms, and the solution of new synthetic problems. These problems are not yet fully recognised, but are dimly perceptible in the quest of complex experiences, in tendencies such as those manifested by artists to reunite arts which have hitherto been differentiated, to federate provinces heretofore entirely foreign to one another. The public is particularly aroused by the performance of productions which have philosophic ideas as a basis, and combine the elements of various arts. Personally I was distinctly conscious of this at the fine rendering of *Prometheus* at the Queen's Hall, London. As I now reflect on the meaning of the war, I am inclined to attribute the public enthusiasm, which touched me so greatly at the time, not so much to the musical side of the work as to its combination of music and mysticism."

Truly the idealist, not the practical man, speaks here. Was he right here as regards the English? I have my doubts.

The war notwithstanding, Scriabin fulfilled his Concert engagements, two in Moscow, one in Charkoff,[1] and three in Petrograd. It was on this last visit to the Northern Capital that his friends noticed with concern that the composer was given to strange moods of depression. But when ques-

[1] Pronounced Harkoff.

tioned he could not account for it, but said that at times he experienced strange forebodings of some grave trouble overhanging him. His last Concert in Petrograd was on April 2, and was a brilliant success. No sooner had he returned to Moscow on Saturday, April 4, than the boil on his lip, from which he suffered so greatly when in London the preceding year and which had been cured by treatment, now appeared again and became exceedingly painful. As it did not improve with medical treatment he cancelled his Volga Concert Tour, which was to have commenced on April 14, 1915. On Tuesday, April 7, Scriabin stayed in bed all day but continued to compose. His temperature began to rise, reaching 40·4 Reamur (123° Fahrenheit). The boil on the lip developed into a carbuncle and blood poisoning set in. During one of his terrible paroxysms of pain, Scriabin's mind flew back to the English people. He would be "more self-possessed," he observed, "like the English." The case defied all medical attention, and it was obvious that things had taken a serious turn. The last rites of the ancient Russian Church were administered, and at five minutes past eight on Tuesday morning, April the 14th, Scriabin passed through that veil which hides the greatest of all the mysteries.

. . . . . .

No sooner was he dead, than the sad news, flashing all over the world, returned to Russia, and his countrymen, oblivious or antagonistic to him all his life, suddenly woke up to the fact that a really great man had passed away beyond their help, and a great national funeral was arranged.

This is ever the reward which the world accords to its great men, whose work must be its own and its sole reward. Scriabin had passed away in the very prime of life, at the age of forty-three, leaving his great undertaking, the *Mystery*, unfinished. This work promised music on higher planes than those hitherto reached,—the opening of new worlds of beauty by the creation of a synthesis of the acoustic, the optical, the choregraphic, and the plastic arts united into one whole by a central mystic and religious idea. This great piece, though conceived throughout in the mind of its creator, was thus left scarcely begun—unfinished and unfinishable.

. . . . . .

On the second day after his death the coffin was brought into the church near his house, and a night vigil was held before a large congregation. Special Anthems were sung by the famous Choir of Alexander Archangelsky. The Funeral Mass took place on April 16, when the famous choir of the Synod-College from the Kremlin, conducted by N. Danilin, sang the music. All the chief Russian musicians, artists, and singers were present. The priest made a touching narration. The funeral procession through the crowded streets was deeply impressive, the coffin being borne for the whole route by the composer's friends and fellow-musicians. A number of young people with linked hands made a chain along the procession, singing the great Russian Anthem for the dead, *Eternal Peace to him.*

. . . . . .

Go out to the Sparrow Hills after a shower of rain has cleared the air of the dust which is such a scourge to Moscow. A scene, like some multi-coloured and fantastic picture out of a fairy book, rises before you—Moscow with its hundreds of glittering domes and cupolas; white walls everywhere, interspersed with restful green patches of foliage; a mighty river trailing its way majestically through the picture with blissful unconcern for the city and its doings. Such was the Moscow which Napoleon saw from the hills in 1812—the promised land which he did not enter. Such too is the picture seen to-day. Near at hand in the foreground stands an exceedingly picturesque Monastery, beautifully situated on the banks of the river. This imposing pile, known as the Devitschy Monastery, has a wonderful history. It was built in 1524 by the fraudulent Duke Vassily III (father of Ivan the Terrible) in commemoration of his conquest of Smolensk.

When the grandson Feodor died, Feodor's widow, Irena, came here for shelter and refuge, and with her came her brother, Boris Godunoff. Boris schemed for and secured the kingdom. Here Peter the Great incarcerated his masterful and rebellious sister Sophia. He lodged her in this Nunnery, had her hair shorn off, and she became Sister Susanna.

The building almost perished in 1812, for Napoleon had it undermined, and the brave intrepid nuns only saved it at the risk of their lives. Part of this old fortress-monastery is now used as a Convent for Girls.

. . . . . .

In a beautiful cloister of this monastery in April, 1915, was seen a wonderful mound of flowers, surmounted by a cross. This is the grave of Alexander Scriabin, whom posterity will assuredly number amongst Russia's very greatest composers—one whom Russia often treated badly in his lifetime, but to whom she seems to have done ample justice in his burial by interring him in this beautiful maiden cloister.

. . . . . .

A sympathetic Moscow lady ended a monograph on the departed one at the time by quoting Tennyson :

> " O well for him whose will is strong;
> He suffers, but he will not suffer long;
> He suffers, but he cannot suffer wrong."

. . . . . .

Immediately after his death his fame increased doubly. Memorial Concerts were given in many cities, and his works appeared in Concerts all over the globe. Especially remarkable was the cycle of orchestral Concerts organised in Moscow by the famous conductor Kussevitzsky. The first Concert took place on October 12, the programme of which was devoted entirely to Scriabin's works. The *First Symphony* was performed with a large chorus, the solo *rôles* in the Hymn to Art being beautifully sung by Miss O. Pavlova (Contralto) and by Mr. J. Altschevsky (Tenor). The *Third Symphony* (*The Divine Poem*) received a magnificent performance. The solo part in the Scriabin *Piano Concerto* was played by Rachmaninoff. A series of Piano Recitals was also given, at which various Moscow pianists devoted themselves entirely to Scriabin's work. Nicolas Orloff played the early compositions. A. Borovsky included the melancholy *Ninth Sonata* in his programme, finishing with the *Third*, which, though also rather sad, ends with a joyful *Finale*. Constantine Igoumnoff, a Professor at the Conservatoire, gave the *Second Sonata*, whilst Alexander Goldenweiser played the mystic, celestial *Tenth*.

At the closing concert of the series, Kussevitzsky conducted the *Second Symphony*, the *Poem of Ecstasy* and *Prometheus*. Kussevitzsky's grasp of Scriabin's work is founded on a close friendship with the composer. He obtains a wonderful attack from his orchestra, and his renderings are characterised by a remarkable fire and rhythmic flow. With him too, as with Scriabin, Art is no mere ornament—but a great and serious responsibility.

. . . . . .

It is comparatively easy to give a rough estimate of Scriabin's character as one reads it from his life's story and music. All his life he was a man of extremes, passionate and tender, impetuous and sensitive. His nature was very affectionate. He was deeply attached to his father, to his foster-mother, "dear Aunt Luboff," and more recently to the two young children he leaves behind. Such a nature is peculiarly sensitive to rebuff or unkindness, which his self-esteem as an artist did not allow him to show. There is no doubt that he felt the opposition of his own country people in Moscow very keenly. Of a retiring disposition like Brahms, with something of a taste for lonely meditation, he lived quietly away from the noisy crowd which were ever agog with greed of office or pecuniary emoluments. He loved small appreciative circles of specially gifted and sympathetic friends, rather than the loud applauding crowd with noisy hands. He was very fortunate with his friends, young and old, whom he never estranged.

The gaudy opera had no attractions for him, and his highly original and imaginative cast of mind revolted against the dry routine of teaching and all that was humdrum and lifeless in conventional life. He was ever the fearless seeker after the inner truth, the brilliant discoverer of new untrodden ways. Even in his childhood, he always preferred his own method, however toilsome, to the generally accepted way.

With great qualities of heart and mind, of a lovable disposition in general, he possessed an unusually fine æsthetic sense; that sense which we

English people are so loth to trust. He was endowed with a wonderfully refined sense of hearing, never more highly developed; he had also a marvellously retentive memory for music and great powers of assimilation.

But perhaps the most outstanding feature to us is his absolute devotion to art, which with him was one with religion. Like his dear, simple, old master Taneieff he found the solution of his existence in life and work, in a blending of life, art, and religion into one. He would at once have agreed with Balfour in his Gifford lectures, where he remarks that all great art must be founded on some system of theism. The fact that never once did Scriabin follow the now almost universal custom of a super-inscribed dedication to some one or other with whom the composer is connected in an affectionate, sentimental, or alas even business-like way, is very significant. No star-conductor finds his name inscribed at the head of Scriabin Symphonies as an inducement for him to cultivate the piece, nor even do any of the smaller pieces bear any of those sentimental dedications which form interesting human documents only in the case of a Beethoven.

There is a story in England of a certain English Bishop who was asked to accept the dedication title of one of those millions of English banalities, commonly called Church Services, which every organist feels inspired (save the mark!) to write. His reply was enlightening. "Is it not already dedicated?"

With Scriabin right from his *First Symphony*—a Hymn of Art where the voices sing—

> " Pure symbols of the Living God,
> Sublimest art of Harmony,
> We raise our fervent hearts to Thee
> In wonder at thy melody,"—

right to his very last piece, all was dedicated to the simple duty of expressing the very best and highest aspirations in him. Even the dance-movements which he inherited from Chopin were turned in his later works into the general stream of praise and delight in creative life.

As an artist he was exceptionally refined and detached, a passionate lover of the beautiful in everything, an ardent devotee of " line " and " design " in art. From the age of twenty-one, when he gradually freed himself from the musical influences which his marvellous powers of assimilation had grafted into his art, he was singularly detached in his artistic view of music. He appeared little interested in the music of others, and entirely wrapped up in his own fascinating ideas of the Unities and of the Ideal in art. I once knew an organist who told me he never went to hear other people play for " fear of contaminating his own style." I can well imagine that Scriabin often kept away from other music for fear of contaminating his own.

On one occasion he was ignorantly accused by a leading Russian critic of being Germanophile. But where he was not Russian he was essentially French in sympathy, style, and in language. He spoke very little English, this fact itself being the mark of the Frenchman rather than of the German, who as a rule speaks it well. All his titles appear in French as well as in Russian, and *only one has a German title.* This is unusual even with the musical "Russian of the Russians."

VII

THE EARLY WORKS

BEETHOVEN strewed his wonderful works and thoughts over the whole collection of musical instruments in use at his time; so too did Bach. Chopin confined himself solely to the piano; whilst the orchestra and the piano alone occupied the attention of Scriabin, who wrote no vocal pieces at all. The small chorus *rôles* in the first and last symphonic works hardly count in this connection. But whilst Scriabin was a wonderful master of orchestration, he cannot be said to have widened its scope to any great extent, as he certainly did with pianoforte technique. Himself a wonderful pianist, he was constantly pushing the limitations farther back, with his playing as with his composition. We cannot fail to notice this as we proceed.

The first five *Opus* numbers need not concern us long. They were written during Scriabin's studentship at the Moscow Conservatoire, and at once show us the great hold which the Polish composer Chopin exercised over the young Russian pianist. Valses, Études, Preludes, Mazurkas—all are clever and original in melody, but everything is clearly seen through Chopin's mind. What a delightful little miniature that early Prelude in B major, Op. 2, No. 2, is! I often play it on the organ. Just a couple of notes on the pedals is all that it requires. Op. 3 consists of *Ten Mazurkas;* they contain many original and piquant little touches. The *Allegro Appassionata*, Op. 4, shows what a command the young musician of seventeen already possessed over harmony and form.

The *First Sonata*, F minor, Op. 6, carries us a stage forward. The whole of Scriabin's art work is so perfectly evolutionary in character, in mastery of technique, in plasticity of musical structure, and in depth of expression,—that any attempt to divide his work into definite periods must be discountenanced. The off-handed saying of some ill-informed professional musicians that Scriabin had two styles—the old and the new—is misleading. Scriabin's final achievements, completely revolutionary in character as they appear when faced singly, were all approached through a perfectly natural and logical development. Once he had planted his feet on his own way—his own musical expression, he freed himself from the influences of the great men who had gone before. This took place about Op. 19 (*Second Sonata*), written in 1880 at the age of eighteen. From this point, free of all trammels, he started forth on the quest which called imperatively to him, and continued steadfastly to the end, never making any concession to the public. Some of our recent geniuses, after a wonderful development of modernity, have dropped back suddenly (as though appalled) to an earlier manner. This was impossible to such as Scriabin, who died in the full zenith of his powers in 1915.

. . . . .

To those who feel somewhat lost among the four hundred odd pieces, large and small, which Scriabin contributed to instrumental music, I would offer the following rough divisions with considerable diffidence :

Opp. 1 to 18. The Apprenticeship works, but still worthy of full respect, since they are all highly finished pieces never betraying a " prentice hand."

Opp. 19 to 40. (*Second Sonata*) to about Op. 50. These works show the full personality on the old lines.

Opp 41 to 52. The Transition period. Works of wonderful beauty and inspiration.

Opp. 53 to 74. The full consummation of Scriabin's genius.

To return to the *First Sonata*, which was written in Moscow in 1889, at the age of seventeen. It is Chopinesque in feeling, truly enough ; but there is a masterly stride in it which even the Polish composer did not possess. It is the music of the Pole combined with the constructive perfection of Brahms. There are, however, many individual touches, and already we cannot fail to see that here is no ordinary musical talent (see Chapter X).

After this Sonata come *Preludes—Preludes—Preludes*. In his later years he preferred the title *Poem*, for this only Prelude, Poem, or Sonata all mean very little. A Sonata may be anything; so may a Poem or a Prelude. It is the contents which counts. To sum up these early pieces quite briefly there will be found in Opp. 7 to 18 abundant material for the concert-room, for the salon, or for the study—a mass of music which will last many pianists the whole of their lives. Everyone should know these works. They are full of fancy, delight, and beauty. They contain reminiscences of gay times in Paris, Amsterdam, and Heidelberg—records of journeys; Op. 11, Nos. 12, 17, 18, and 23 all written at Vitzau on Lake Lucerne in 1885; No. 14 at Dresden; souvenirs of holidays in Kieff (1889), and experiments in all sorts of curious times and in unusual figuration.

Dr. Terry thus describes the *Twelve Études*, Op. 8:

"No. 1 is Schumannesque, but with real fire and richness. No. 2 is certainly Chopin, but more incisively rhythmic; quite straightforward and diatonic, with a striking *pianissimo* ending to its fiery vigour. No. 3 might be termed a 'Moto perpetuo,' its strong right-hand melody dominating the tempestuous triplet accompaniment. No. 4 has a truly ravishing melody as Chopinesque as No. 2 in tonality and treatment, but with an individuality all its own. The exultant and confident freedom of No. 5 brings us to the rather uneventful No. 6, with its running sixths—perhaps more suggestive of Chopin than any of the others. No. 7 I do not find particularly interesting, but it is certainly not dull. To my mind the most interesting numbers are 9, 10, and 12. No. 8 is interesting and quite straightforward; the right-hand melody a little conventional, but its alternation with solemn chords (in the familiar style of a Chopin Nocturne) relieves it of monotony. It is in No. 9 that one first seems to get a glimpse of the later Scriabin. It opens with a fiery outburst as of one exulting in the pride of strength. The broadly tranquil opening of its second section is strongly suggestive of the slow stirring of a giant's limbs as he wakes refreshed, calmly exultant in his strength, passing swiftly to action like a young Siegfried, as the torrent of life surges through his veins. The running thirds in No. 10 again recall Chopin, but the resistless energy of the whole piece carries one away. It quivers with the joy of life—the life of fresh winds and sun and sea. A more sober mood entered with the sonorous bass figure towards the very end. No. 11 is marked by a brooding tenderness that is never sombre, though the 'uneasy' chords at the end create a certain atmosphere of apprehensiveness, as though some sinister idea had obtruded itself. But it is in No. 12 that the sure grip of the composer comes out strongest. Broad and majestic in its opening phrases, it passes as swiftly through as many moods as No. 9, now surging passionately like a soul scaling celestial heights, now soaring in calm ecstasy on pinions of song. It is a foretaste of that marvellous unveiling of a human soul which his later Sonatas show."

Op. 9, *Prelude and Nocturne for the Left Hand only*, reminds us of the marvellous development of his left-hand part in all his keyboard music, and it also recalls the period in his early teens when a broken right shoulder-blade compelled him to practise impatiently all his music with his left hand alone.

I return to Dr. Terry's article in the *Music Student* for a description of Op. 11:

"These *Twenty-four Preludes* are all of them short, ten of surpassing beauty, and most of them a great advance on Op. 8. No. 1 is dainty and all too brief. No. 2 more pensive; much of it is in the nature of a duet between the two hands, and the recurring right-hand figure is a thing of beauty. Nos. 3, 4, and 5 have great distinction; the first is a *Presto* movement of 'Spinning-wheel' type, and is perfectly exquisite; the second foreshadows the deep brooding of later compositions; slow and solemn, it speaks of perplexity, of puzzled expectancy. There is no

Schumann or Chopin here; he has found his own language. No. 5 somewhat resembles the preceding one in mood but not in structure; it has greater confidence and ends tranquilly; again the melodic figure is perfect. No. 6 is impetuous, and strangely resembles Schumann's well-known Novellette in D; the rhythmic figures are quite as straightforward. No. 8 is very dainty, but bears little stamp of Scriabin's own personality; it might easily pass for pure Chopin.

"Nos. 9 and 10 stand out with a dignity all their own. The former opens with noble simplicity. It is full, rich, and warm-coloured, the sonorous left-hand figure contributing in no small degree to this effect. It is the perfect expression of the dignity of a strong and simple soul. No. 10 has all the sonorous breadth of its predecessor, but the mood becomes more intense; it ends with simplicity and sombre pomp. No. 11 gives one the impression of a struggle for expression between Scriabin and Chopin, in which the former eventually obtains the mastery. No. 12 is all Scriabin; one sees his grip of things tightening. The hesitating pauses of the right hand give a curious impression of inconclusive reflections. (This is a constantly recurring feature in Scriabin's later work.) No. 13 is a perfect little picture of tranquil musings; not a note of it suggests Schumann, but the emotional effect, so far as the present writer is concerned, was strangely like that produced by his first hearing of Act III of Schumann's *Faust* (where 'Pater

Ecstaticus' speaks). No. 14 is triumphant and masterful. Both in construction and effect it strongly suggests the *Ride of the Valkyries.* In this and also in the two following pieces one feels Scriabin has reached a higher plane of thought and expression than in any previous work. No. 15 seems to be asking a perpetual question—Where? Whither?—but it is all so sane and hopeful. In this, as in all Scriabin, I see nothing decadent or neurotic. No. 16 is marked 'Misterioso,' but I confess to finding less mystery about it than restrained sonority, and the glow of Oriental colouring. To me it came as the first piece of Scriabin where one could truly say, 'Here is the Slav.' An odd echo of the opening of Chopin's funeral march sounds like an intrusion. No. 17 is simple and undistinguished. No. 18 is rather savagely impetuous, quite pianistic, and suggests no particular train of thought.

"No. 19 is a noble number indeed. There is at length that greater sonority and wealth of both rhythmic and harmonic material which distinguishes the later Scriabin, but again we have those odd intrusions of Chopinesque turns of expression (both rhythmic and melodic). The Chopin idiom is being shaken off, but it still peeps in at odd moments. No. 20 suggests the mood of No. 18, in its strepitant opening, but it gradually subsides like a spent wave. It is a fine number, though very short. No. 21 is a melody in the right hand with arpeggio accompaniment in the left. The last traces of Schumann seem to be ebbing away here. It is a piece of sheer beauty and the mood is contented and serene. No. 22 is likewise very beautiful. It opens in the same mood as its predecessor, but with fuller chords and warmer colouring; it later develops agitation, and finally the now familiar subsidence into contented weariness—all this in the short space of 24 bars. No. 23 is as dainty as Chopin at his daintiest, but with the Scriabin grip and individuality now. No. 24 is rather larger than most, and surges along with tempestuous energy and force."

Op. 19 brings us to the *Second Sonata*, a "Fantasy Sonata." The two movements, although written at different times, coalesce spiritually in such a wonderful way. The first movement (*Andante*) was written at Genoa in 1892; the second, five years later in the Crimea. Does the equal geographical latitude account for the cohesion? An interesting question! There are three chief themes in the first movement, all of great beauty: the first subject, very striking in rhythmical importance; the second, a gracefully spun melodic line, and the third an aspiring hymn-like tune. Also the composer, as is his wont, elevates his bridge-passage almost into a new subject, thus making four themes for this highly finished and very eloquent movement. The last three notes of the first subject are significant, as the little motive appears to have obsessed Scriabin's mind all his life. They are like the "Knocks of Fate" in

Beethoven, and are used at various points throughout the movement. This trait was destined to become a regular feature of Scriabin's works. The second (and final) movement *Presto* has three subjects—two of graceful filigree work, whilst the third—to which he evidently attaches most importance—is a hymn-like melody of great nobility and beauty.

The Piano Concerto, Opus 20

In originality and imagination I place the *Second Sonata* far above the *Pianoforte Concerto*, which is perhaps the most popular of all Scriabin's pianoforte works. This *Concerto in F sharp*, Op. 20, was completed shortly after taking over his duties as Professor of Pianoforte Playing in his *alma mater*, the Moscow Conservatoire, in 1897. It is in three movements: an *Allegro* in F sharp minor, 3–4 time; an *Andante* in F sharp major, 4–4; and an *Allegro* in F sharp minor and major, 9–8 time. This novel return to the uni-tonality of the old Suite form is noteworthy. The first movement has subjects of great beauty handled with exquisite artistry, but is perhaps a little lacking in melodic development. The *Andante* (nearer *Adagio* surely, for it is marked 46 to the crotchet) is a set of charming variations on one of the loveliest themes ever penned. This hymn-like melody of 16 bars, played *con sordino*, is tinted with the ethereal beauty of the *Adagio* in the 12th Quartet of Beethoven.

The *Finale*, an *Allegro Moderato*, is a little weak

in thematic material and handling until it reaches the *Meno Allegro*, when the second (or is it the third ?) subject is given out in F major with light palpitating chords on the piano, whilst the wood-wind breathe pale-coloured mists in the background. The movement increases in interest as we proceed until a magnificent climax is reached with the return of the second subject in the Tonic major. The work is redolent of Chopin, but undoubtedly possesses decided individuality ; and the handling of form and of the orchestra is far in advance of that of the great Pole. We must not blame Scriabin for his unstinted admiration of the greatest master of the genius of the piano, and indeed it would be one of the greatest tributes to call him "The Russian Chopin," just as Medtner is frequently styled "The Russian Brahms." But it would only express a part of the truth in Scriabin's case, for he is much more than this.

The *First* and *Second Symphonies* followed the *Third Sonata.* No. 1, in E major, has a Choral Epilogue—a "Hymn to Art." It was written during the six years which Scriabin seems to have wasted as Professor of the Pianoforte Class at his *alma mater*—from 1897 to 1903. During these six years he hardly composed anything, but he completed his *Second Symphony* in 1903 shortly after his resignation from the tutorial staff. Two earlier pieces of considerable importance are the *Fastasia in B*, Op. 28, and the Tragedy (*Poème Tragique*), Op. 34. The Fantasia is a piece on full symphonic lines, with an exposition of three subjects well contrasted ; the first of a noble melancholy :

the second of an exquisite tenderness :

the third of a majestic grandeur:

There is a most masterly development and a full Return with a grandiose Coda. The only drawback is its difficulty, for here we no longer have the sketchiness of keyboard music which satisfied Beethoven and even Brahms in the more extended parts, but a full three-handed setting all to be encompassed by those wonderful, yet often wooden, ten fingers of ours.

The *Tragedy*, Op. 34, one of his finest pieces, seems to represent some popular festivity on a grand scale into the middle of which has come some striking tragedy which awes and astounds. The festivities are then resumed with the original vigour.

Op. 33 is an interesting set, containing four little impressions of some of the chief prevailing moods in Scriabin's richly endowed emotional temperament. No. 1, the dance emotion ; No. 2, the elusive and fanciful meditation, only vaguely defined ; No. 3, the leonine mood, outraged pride ; No. 4, bellicose : To arms ! Anyone interested in the psychological import of Scriabin's music can easily trace all these moods under his continually progressive style. Compare No. 3 here, for instance,

with Op. 37, No. 4 ; Op. 56, No. 1 ; Op. 59, No. 2 ; and so on.

The year 1903 was amazingly fruitful in works, being probably the most fertile period of Scriabin's life. In the space of nine months, he wrote all the pieces from Opp. 30 to 43, including the *Fourth Sonata*, the Third Symphony (*The Divine Poem*), and a large number of Études, Preludes, Valses, and Poems. There is only room here to mention a few of these pieces. Let us choose the set of Preludes, Op. 31, the brilliant *Poème Satanique*, Op. 36, and the *Four Preludes*, Op. 37.

The First Prelude of the four in Op. 31 is a slow, sweet melody in D flat, delicious in its curves and long-drawn breaths. The overlapping accompaniment figure, which he so much affected, is frequently found also in the piano works of his old tutor, Taneieff. It commences in D flat, but ends in C major.

I give a couple of bars because the left-hand work is a permanent characteristic of Scriabin :

The second, marked *con stravagante* (*Anglicè :* let yourself go), is a fine example of the little Prelude form, in the sense used by Chopin ; for it is a decided mood-piece with a very passionate Russian outburst of temper. The chord of the " French Sixth " with the Dominant in the Bass is much in evidence ; indeed he seems fairly obsessed with this chord at this period, and I think it was one of the chords which first turned him to the possibilities of the new harmony. Compare this piece, for instance, with the *Poème Satanique*, which is on the border-line of the new harmony, and with the *Ironica* of No. 56, which is well into the new tract.

The *Third Prelude,* Op. 31, is another cross-rhythm piece study in quintuples; whilst the last one is an outstanding little gem of harmonic thought —a delightful little miniature. I have given it in full in Chapter XV of my *Modern Harmony* (Augener, London).

Perhaps the one thing which will retard largely the popularity of Scriabin's pianoforte pieces is the occasional unapproachableness of the technique from the amateur's point of view. Still, whilst many of the pieces in all the three chief styles of Scriabin present great difficulties for either the right hand (as in Op. 37, No. 1); or else for the left (No. 3); if, indeed, not for both (No. 2). Still there is always one piece at least in each Opus more approachable, as for instance No. 4 in this set. It is angry and powerful in mood, and well laid out in design. Yet do not let us get the idea that Scriabin is "unpianistic." No one, not even Chopin, understood and wrote for the piano more entirely in its proper genius than did Scriabin.

VIII

THE WORKS OF THE TRANSITION PERIOD

THE division of Scriabin's work into periods is a somewhat unsatisfying procedure. For instance, there is a *Prelude*, No. 2 in Op. 39, which, although quite short, is full of prophecy of the new stage. It is also, by the way, a real little gem of music. Again, the Op. 36, *Poème Satanique*, is one of the most striking of all his pieces. There we have rugged ironic phrases alternating with tender *cantabile amoroso* melodies. It would seem that Satire and Irony are quite modern additions to music. I do not know the Psychology of Satire, and, though cheap sarcasm seldom serves any fine purpose, satire may at times be very salutary. But music cannot be consistently satirical for long, and even then only through contrast and not otherwise. So the result here is a magnificent piece of music, bellicose, imperious, calm, tender, and winning by turns. We find it in his favourite chord, the "French Sixth," carried one stage further. The final Cadence will serve to illustrate this point:

In Op. 40, *Two Mazurkas,* the first one (marked at a speed no Mazurka is ever danced—168 equals crotchet) has an exquisite charm. It seems a shame to analyse such a piece of fragile beauty; but theoretically it is a study with unusual positions of the chord of the 13th with the minor 9th, and it is specially interesting as a sort of study for the later *Danse caresse,* Op. 57, with which it is closely connected in feeling. There are alternate *languido* and *tempo* bars, and the piece is a perfect little cameo of delicate rhythm.

By the term "Poem" Scriabin seems to indicate a poetical piece longer than a short Prelude or Miniature—a piece with more than one subject. In Op. 41, *Poème in D flat,* we have a softly breathed melody, over a fluttering accompaniment of exquisite delicacy, for the first subject. This forms a strong contrast with the middle portion, where a more impassioned melody is accompanied by agitated downward arpeggios in the Bass. The harmony here points to a forward evolutionary stage. The various "Sets" of Preludes are always more difficult to place in evolution, as it was his custom to write these shorter pieces at different times, whenever the mood struck him, and to gather them up and publish them in sets later on. The first of the *Set of Eight Preludes,* Op. 42, is a fairly long and intricate finger piece. It is also a problem in rhythm—5 crotchets in the bass against 9 quavers in the treble. The second one is also in cross-rhythm. The third is a delicate fluttering *Prestissimo.* They are all good to play and good to hear.

In Op. 44, *Two Poems*, we are decidedly arriving amongst the upper harmonics. The first piece here contradicts my earlier definition of "Poem," for it is very short and has only one subject, a long-drawn song-melody in the clarinet register of the keyboard. The second *Poem* is in ten-bar phrases —an unusual thing with Scriabin.

The *Feuillet d'album*, Op. 45 (i), I find very near the commonplace; but this may only be by contrast with the fantastic charm of the *Poem* (No. 2), and the delicious harmony and appoggiaturas in No. 3 of the same Opus. The fantastic note is again to the fore in the *Scherzo*, Op. 46, but a serious mood comes over the composer just at the finish. In the *Quasi-Valse*, Op. 47, we again see how Scriabin approached the new harmony step by step, through the device of *appoggiaturas* and passing notes.

An impetuous, fiery little *Prelude* opens the 48th Opus. This is followed by a short hymn-like *Adagio* with a delicate web of arpeggio filigree below; by a capricious restless little *Prelude* in D flat (threes against twos), and by a jubilant *Festival Piece* in C, this last, a splendid little tone-picture full of glowing sunlight.

Op. 49, *Three Pieces: Study, Prelude, Reverie*, is a very valuable little set. The Study is the nearest approach to an Æolian harp which I have yet heard.

The *Prelude* is written with the leonine rage which is one of Scriabin's prevailing moods; whilst the *Reverie* is a harmonic Pastel of a tender delicacy. The compositions of the middle period—say roughly from Opp. 34 to 50—are amongst the happiest and serenest things in music. He has lost his youthful love of melancholy, and knows nothing of the almost anxious philosophy of some of the later pieces or the shadowy deeps of the middle Sonatas, without which perhaps his radiant moments might seem less bright. Here in the summer of his life all is radiant happiness, the joying in beauty, in the warmth of friendship, and in the love of a life which he finds good to live. Even on the few occasions when he indulges in Satire (as in *Poème Satanique*) his happier nature wins easily. Play the final *Prelude* in Op. 48 if you want to hear real joy—the shared human joy of Beethoven's *Ninth Symphony*,

> "*Joy, thou daughter of Elysium,*
> *'Tis thy magic art that knitteth*
> *What stern fashion's law would part;*
> *Where thy gentle presence dwelleth,*
> *Men are one in soul and heart.*"[1]

With Scriabin it is all done entirely through the wonders of harmony itself.

[1] Natalia Macfarren's translation (Novello).

IX

THE "MYSTIC CHORD"

"Those men of genius who cannot be surpassed may be equalled. How? By being different."
Victor Hugo.

We know that no musical sound or note is absolutely pure and single.[1] All contain a large number of upper partial tones (some heard, others inaudible) which help to make up the general effect of the ground-tone which we recognise chiefly as the note. Here is the table of those most usually recognised. When the low C is struck, an exceptionally trained ear could doubtless recognise the presence of all these:

If you cannot hear them easily, you can prove their existence by a simple experiment at the piano keyboard. Put the note No. 2 down silently, now strike No. 1 shortly and sharply, and you will hear No. 2 respond, though you have done nothing directly to agitate its wire strings. All the others can be proved in the same way, even Nos. 7, 11 and 13, which are not quite in tune with Nature's chord. (Don't call it Nature's *scale;* because it is a *chord.*)

[1] Except perhaps a very few notes on the flute and on specially prepared metal bars.

But this is not the way the harmony of Palestrina, Purcell, Handel, Bach, and Beethoven was derived. Although many theorists—Rameau, Day, Hiles, Macfarren, and even Prout—have from time to time endeavoured to force the theory of harmony on to these lines, it should be remembered that theorists should follow the artists and not precede them; and even down to the present day, musical composers have shown themselves singularly ignorant of the laws of Acoustics.[1]

Our harmony grew up on far different lines in tentative, æsthetic, and empirical ways. And so too did all our scales. In an illuminating talk I had once with my friend, Dr. Walford Davies, he gave a clever exposition of the way in which he considered our harmony had evolved. Obviously the octave, being the natural distance between the male and female voices, or those of boys and men, would be the first interval discovered. Then a more fastidious choice of a comfortable interval would be the 4th or 5th between. Then the 5th would be divided in its turn; and then the 4th. Larger clusters of notes with added "tones" would be used, until at length the "whole-tone" chords were reached.

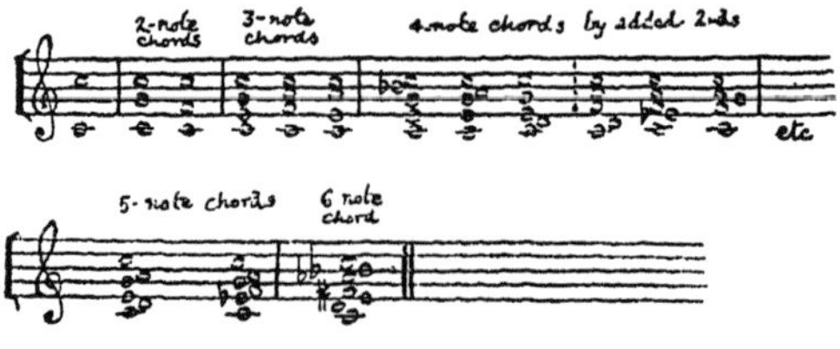

[1] The Belgian theorist d'Ergo points out many discrepancies and falsities in Strauss' revision of Berlioz's "Instrumentation" (Peters).

It is true that now and again the practice of Beethoven, Bach, and all the others does seem to coincide with the laws of Acoustic Science, but whatever be the significance of this, it is only with them for special cases.

(*a*) BEETHOVEN

(*b*) BRAHMS

And even so, these cases all stop short at those upper partial notes which are badly out of tune with our present practical system: Nos. 11, 13, 14, and 15, for instance.

But Scriabin, in his later stages, assumes they are quite near enough for the purpose and takes them all into his net. Moreover, he accepts the whole series, 7ths, 9ths, 13ths, etc., as a *concord*, and in his last period especially cultivates the higher partials even to the most varied placements and inversions. He still regards them as inversions *even when the root is absent*. Further, having accepted the piano tuning (duodecuple) as his basis, he writes these harmonics quite freely as enharmonics. G flat and F sharp and so on, are all the same to him. For instance, Op. 65 (ii) ends in D flat, but is described as being in C sharp. Again in the *Poème Satanique*, where the following :

is repeated, the G flat is more correctly *F sharp*. Later on, in the following chord :

the G sharp is obviously the minor 9th, *A flat*. This

does not sound very consistent with his theory, and it often makes his root troublesome to find. But why bother about it?—Since the two *sounds* are accepted as the same in music, what does the notation matter—or the unknown root either? The music is the thing.

Scriabin founded no new scale. English and American writers have been led astray on this point. He uses the Duodecuple scale, which is that now adopted by all modern writers: Strauss, Elgar, Debussy, Cyril Scott, Ravel, and all the others. He discovered many new chords or combinations; but, what is more remarkable, he invented practically a new style of composition. He takes a certain new chord which suits the particular feelings he wants to express, and evolves the whole composition out of this one extended harmony, using it only on a very few roots, often two or three; sometimes even only one. Moreover, he adopts his series as a perfect concord, satisfying in itself. Debussy, Cyril Scott, and others have done this, but they do not develop on the lines of Scriabin. In his early period Scriabin himself used some of these newer combinations as discords, and resolved them accordingly; and indeed many of these newer chords have been reached in other (empirical) ways by such composers as York-Bowen, Vaughan-Williams, Coleridge-Taylor (*Hiawatha* cadence), and others.

But once Scriabin has chosen a particular combination for a piece, he adopts it whole-heartedly—and the perfect revolution in music that it involves.

The old major and minor modes go; the key-signature goes (not the tonality); and the "equal temperament" in tuning is accepted in a way never entirely done before (despite Bach's "Forty-eight"). His chosen "foundation chord," sweet sounding or not, is accepted as a concord, and the only discords left then are "suspensions," "passing notes," and "appoggiaturas."

He chooses any sounds he likes from the "harmonic series" (Ex. 8), and arranges them for the purpose as he fancies. One chord, which his disciples have dubbed the "mystic chord," is a selection from the first thirteen of this series, arranged in a structure of 4ths. There is no mystery about it. It is wonderfully logical. He simply says: "Take the sounds from the natural series and build them up in a structure of 4ths." The result is a chord of extreme beauty and interest:

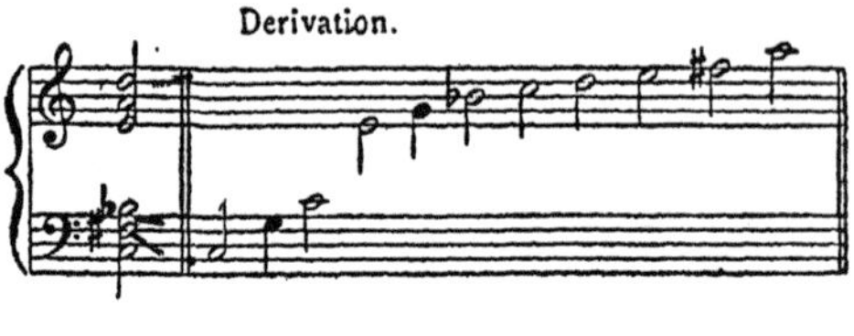

Play it over *forte*, then *piano*; then sprinkle it very softly; try it in various keys. We have the splendid vitality of the augmented 4th, the soft mollity of the diminished 4th, the sweet firmness of the perfect 4th, and so on. Reckoning everything from the root, we get the "augmented

11th," the "minor 7th," the 3rd, the 13th, and the 9th. The marvellous possibilities of such a chord are seen in *Prometheus*, the *Seventh Sonata*, the *Feuillet d'album*, Op. 58, etc., which are all founded on this one chord alone. Common chords, 7ths, 6–5's, augmented 6ths, even the "whole-tone" scale are only a few of the derivatives of such a far-reaching chord. Long passages in 9ths, 7ths, or 5ths all spring from it quite naturally. (See Op. 65, Nos. 1, 2, 3.)

For other pieces Scriabin takes simpler combinations. The two pieces in Op. 57 are founded on this chord :

Of course the chords appear in any arrangement of the notes, 4ths, 3rds, 2nds, etc., and even when arranged in his chief position—in 4ths, the root may be scarcely touched, as in *Étrangeté* (see following Ex.), or in Op. 59 (ii), the opening of the Tenth Sonata, or the last chords of Op. 63 (ii) and 65 (iii).

On the other hand, we find some very complex and puzzling "concords" in the later pieces. Op. 65 (ii) is constructed on the following:

The *Sixth Sonata* is founded on the following wondrous combination: G, C, F, B, and E flat. The Sonata is in G—or rather *on* G:

The mysterious *Seventh Sonata* is evolved from one harmony only, even the second chord being the same as the first with the omission of one of the notes.

The Sonata is a marvel of development from a single harmony. Tone-clangs, tollings of every colour and emotion, subjects, counter-subjects, even the following lovely theme of comparative consonance may be found amongst the upper partials :

The *Eighth Sonata* is founded on the following foundation chord :

No. 4 in the final set of *Preludes* ends with this remarkable chord:

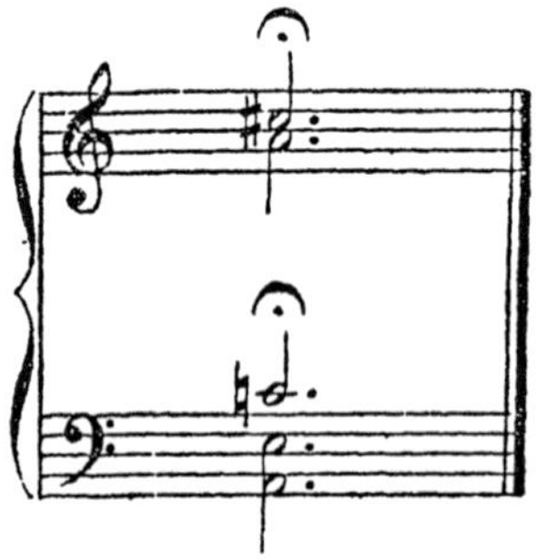

Sometimes, the whole composition is evolved from one chosen combination; but more often two combinations (sometimes only differing by one note) are selected for variety. Occasionally the first subject is founded on one harmony; the second subject being built on another, as in *Étrangeté*, Op. 69.

Sometimes he lets his combination oscillate slightly in some part. As in the Prelude, Op. 6, No. 2, where the E flat finally decides on E natural at the close.

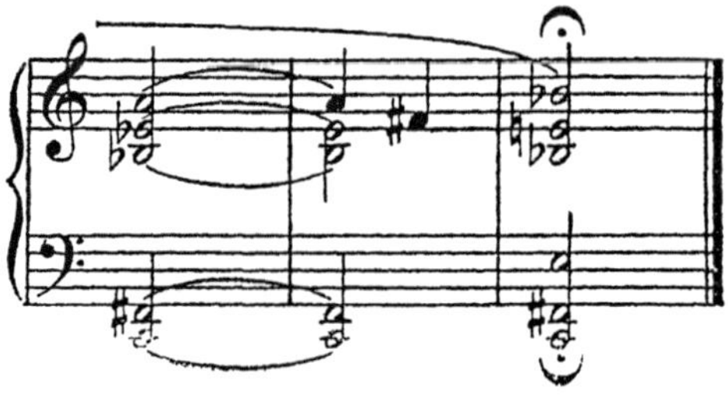

When three chords are selected, we frequently find this formula A, B, A, C.

His Bass progressions are much simpler as a rule than in the ordinary practice of other composers. Occasionally he is satisfied with two basses only, and then the choice falls invariably on the augmented 4th (or diminished 5th), which in Scriabin may be regarded as the Dominant. See Op. 56 (iv), the *Étude*, Op. 65 (iii), the *Poem*, Op. 69, the piece Op. 58 in the *New Russian Album*, etc.

The preference for this progression in the Bass is seen even in the earlier pieces of his older style in the *Mazurka*, Op. 40 (i), in the *Scherzo*, Op. 46, the *Quasi Valse*, Op. 47, etc. Rachmaninoff, by the way, was not impervious to the beauty of this harmonic colouring. Witness the following passage from his *Elegy :*

Occasionally the Bass steps by major 3rds (Op. 67, ii); sometimes by minor 3rds, as in *Masque*, Op. 63 (i), *Étude*, Op. 66 (i), *Prélude*, Op. 67 (i), *Vers la Flamme*, Op. 72, etc.; and even by major 2nds or diminished 3rds (Op. 65, i and ii; Op. 67, i). When we find the ordinary Tonic and Dominant progression in the Bass as in the *Désir* and the *Danse caresse*, the music is much easier to understand. The perfect equality of the steps of the above-mentioned progressions in the Bass should be carefully noticed, as I think much of the strangeness of Scriabin's music is due to it. I have noted this before in the works of Ravel, Karg-Elert, Reger, Cyril Scott, Bantock, Tscherepnine, even in Wagner, and in my *Modern Harmony*, I theorised to some extent on this subject, long before I knew that Scriabin's practice supported my theory.

. . . . . .

Let us now take a couple of pieces and analyse them from this point of view.

Poem, Op. 52 (i) in C. Two harmonies only are used for this Ex., (*a*) and (*b*):

In bar I we have (*a*), in bars 2–3 (*b*), in bar 4 (*a*)

again; in bar 5 the (*a*) chord over A flat root; in bars 6–7 (*a*) chord over F root. This swings us to a new centre, D instead of C, which device is the nearest to a modulation which Scriabin can make on these new lines. Bars 8 to 14 are the first seven bars transposed a note higher. Bars 16 to 24 show the (*b*) series gradually swinging itself down on a long G pedal-point. Then the whole piece repeats itself with transposition, ending over a long C pedal-point, varied by occasional interposed A flat chords. The piece closes with a common chord. It belongs to the transitional period.

Prelude in C, Op. 59 (ii), savage and bellicose, is founded on the following modified series of 4ths.

In (*a*) we have the major 7th omitted; in (*b*) it is present, but the augmented 4th is replaced by the 5th. The theme (bars 1–5) is founded on these two chords; it is then transposed a minor 3rd up (6–10), the (*b*) series is then augmented in time duration and dwelt on at considerable length, bringing out all its most aggressive qualities (bars 11–26). We see in bars 14–15, etc., how an ordinary plain common chord may be derived from such a complex series.

The rest of the piece is mere transposition, the alternating chord on C being constructed with the omission of one note (A) and substitution of the fifth (G) for F sharp.

There is not a sop for the conservatives even in the final chord, which is constructed thus :

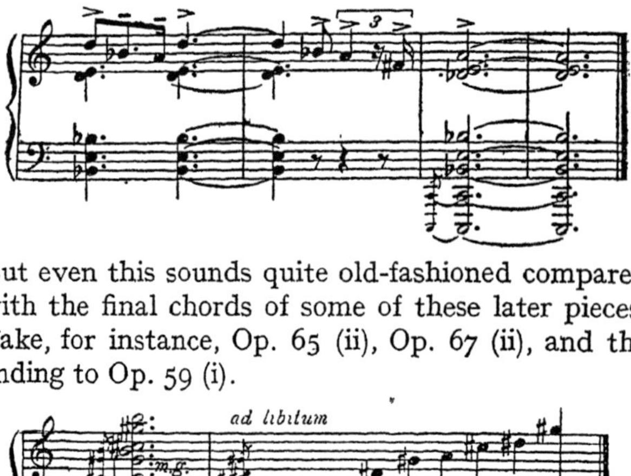

But even this sounds quite old-fashioned compared with the final chords of some of these later pieces. Take, for instance, Op. 65 (ii), Op. 67 (ii), and the ending to Op. 59 (i).

Advanced as all this sounds, it is still a logical growth from the earlier elaboration made possible by the sustaining pedal to Field, and afterwards to Chopin, and finally to Scriabin. Thinking entirely along these lines, we might sketch out briefly the history of harmonic evolution there thus :

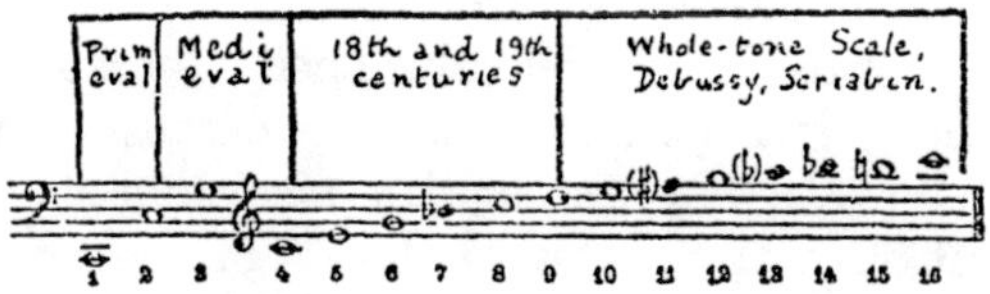

But how much better such harmony sounds on the yielding evanescent and ethereal tones of the piano than on the very irregularly constituted tone-productions of the modern orchestra. The subject is too vast to pursue further here ; but I am opening it up in a new book, *Further Studies in Modern Harmony*.

X

THE TEN SONATAS

We have elsewhere emphasised the perfectly natural growth and evolutionary character of Scriabin's creations. As one proceeds onwards, from the earliest pieces of his childhood and student days at Moscow to the stage when he finds his own individuality on the old lines; then again through the transition period, when we find him pushing out as it were tentatively here and there in his rhythm, in his handling of themes, in his texture, but especially in his harmony; right up to the culmination of his new style in the final works—we always find a step forward into new terrain with each successive piece. Nowhere is this feature better seen than with the *Ten Sonatas*, which reveal themselves as so many landmarks in the evolution of Scriabin's style and expression.

But this is by no means the only (nor the chief) recommendation of these Sonatas to special notice; for in the judgment of most modern critics they are in every way worthy of ranking with the very greatest things in pianoforte literature. They are destined in the future to occupy a niche of their own, together with such treasures as the *Forty-eight Fugues* of Bach, the *Thirty-two Sonatas* of Beethoven, the Pianoforte Works of Brahms, and the music of Chopin.

These *Ten Sonatas* were written at various periods spread over the whole of his artistic career. In them we see the Russian composer as a harmonic revolutionary; and at the same time as a thoroughgoing conservative in the matter of instrumental form and design.

Following strictly in his middle period upon the lines laid down by Beethoven, Scriabin, even in his later Sonatas, approximates the principles of Beethoven's forms to the application of Liszt's method of using themes.

The First Sonata, F minor, Opus 6

What a beginning we find here! The young musical giant commences with an Olympian stride comparable only to that of Brahms in his *Sonata in F minor*, Op. 5. Scriabin's *First Sonata* was written in Moscow in 1892, shortly after the termination of his course at the Conservatoire. It was published by M. P. Belaieff in 1895. As may be expected in a first work, there are traces of outside influence, chiefly of Chopin. But the Polish tone-poet was never such a perfect writer of musical form as we find here. There are abundant traces of a rising individuality, chiefly in certain distinctive melodic turns, in the handling of the subjects, in the texture of the accompaniment-figures, in the dispersion of his chords, and in his rhythmical patterns.

The Sonata is in three movements. The first movement is in the so-called "Sonata form," with its exposition of three subjects; then their development; the final recapitulation and the coda. The first theme commences as follows:

The bridge portion begins at the end of the eighth bar, and leads in the twenty-first bar to the second subject (*meno mosso*) in the key of E flat major. The individual poetic note of the young musician comes out very strongly here.

At bar 41 we have a third subject in the key of A flat which finishes with a perfect cadence.

After a few beats' rest the "development" (45 bars in all) commences with the first subject in the enharmonic key of G sharp minor. The strenuous third subject now appears, *muted*, with its rhythm dully thudding in the bass. The first subject increases the effect of its soaring nature by being developed in the major mode. But this suddenly evaporates into the little motive of its first three notes, sadly predictive of the Funeral March at the end of the Sonata. This, however, is soon brushed aside; the first subject resumes its soaring, and suddenly bursts into the return of the first Exposition, here appearing with the utmost force. The second subject likewise appears brilliantly displayed in C minor with widely-spread chords of great strength. A soft Dominant Pedal-point brings in the third subject in F major, with its rising scale progression. The majesty gradually disappears in the last eight bars, where there is a curious vacillation between the major and minor—between the moods of optimism and pessimism. But the mood of the whole movement is that of a noble aspiration.

The second movement is in Song form. The first theme is the very quintessence of the folk-song spirit—highly idealised. It consists of four phrases, commencing thus:

The second subject is founded on the fundamental germ of the Sonata.

This reaches a certain stage of aspiration, and then melts into the reappearance of the first (folk-song) subject—this time with a busy restless bass figuration. A charming movement, full of wonderful beauty!

The third (final) movement (*presto*) is constructed over a musical framework known as the "Rondo-Sonata" form. The first subject appears over the little palpitating figure in the bass. This figure also is derived from the fundamental motive.

The second subject appears in bar 13. We then hark back to the first, which gives in its turn to the second subject of the *first* movement, which is considerably expanded here. The first subject again intervenes; then the second subject, and finally the first again, the music culminating rapidly in force and leading to—sudden disaster (*Marche Funèbre*). This is relieved in the middle by an angelic song of celestial beauty, *quasi mente* (in the distance).

What a work for a beginning—filled doubtless with that pessimism to which youth turns so glibly between eighteen and twenty-one—but filled also with an immense strength—a spirit evidently prepared to battle with "the sorry scheme of things." If aspiration be the key-note of the first movement, and the pleasure of poetic dreamy meditation of the second, then a sudden girding on of strength ready for the dimly-felt on-coming disaster is the keynote of the third.

There is a fixed unity of purpose about the whole work; and the tragedy of it strangely predicts and summarises the story of the composer's life. There are many other technical and artistic unifying devices which bind the whole work together in a closer embrace than we find with Beethoven—devices learnt from Brahms; the construction and the transmutation of the themes from Liszt. The first subject of the first movement, the second subject of the second, the first subject of the *finale* and the Funeral March are all built from the same little three-note germ.

Compare the fateful knocking too, just before the Angelic Song in the Funeral March, and its re-appearance in the last bar of the Sonata. It has some affinity with the "Fate theme" of Beethoven's *Fifth Symphony*; but here, it is as though young Scriabin, like the Eastern philosopher, impatiently "turned up an empty glass."

The Second (Fantasy) Sonata, G sharp minor, Opus 19

This Sonata is in two movements only. The first movement was begun by Scriabin at Genoa in 1892, but the second movement was not written until 1897 when he was in the Crimea. The Sonata was published by M. P. Belaieff in 1898. The composer has here completely found his whole individuality, and in depth of thought and expression and mastery of presentation, it leaves the *First Sonata* far behind. The first movement is marked *Andante*, but metronomed at 60 to the crotchet.[1] The second is a *Presto* in 3–2 time. There is no actual thematic relationship between the two movements.[2] But there is a close spiritual relationship of Question and Answer—a Proposition and its exact complement. The two movements are also subtly connected by the key-scheme; thus the Sonata opens in G sharp minor in the orthodox form—but the whole of the usual "Recapitulation part" (much condensed) appears in the unusual key of E major. This runs into the last movement without break—the final movement (*Presto*) being in the original Tonic minor key (G sharp minor).

We will now look at the movements more in detail. The first movement (*Andante*) is constructed in the usual Sonata-form. The first theme is striking.

It bears a subtle relationship with the "knocks of Fate" in Beethoven's *Fifth Symphony*. For the "bridge-subject" the first subject is transformed,

[1] Mendelssohn's use of the term *Andante* is similarly misleading. The Italian word simply means "walking," "going," or "moving."

[2] Unless it be between the three repeated notes in the first bar of the opening and the three reiterated ninths in the left hand of the subsidiary theme *dolcissimo* of the second movement (page 13).

leading to the "second theme" (bar 23) (in the regulation relative key, B major).

Already we see a liking for the soft effect of the major 2nd in chord formation. Of course they are here taken as appoggiaturas, but nearly all the newer chords were discovered in this way.

This is surrounded with filigree work of great poetic beauty, especially on its immediate repetition, which gradually makes way for the third subject—a hymn-like melody (also in B major) of strong melodic charm and much nobility.

The "Exposition" ends at the fifty-seventh bar with a "full close" in B major.[1] A short but masterly development follows (29 bars in all), dealing with the first and second subjects (not the third), and especially with the "fateful knockings." The "Recapitulation" section is noteworthy. Two bars only of the first subject suffice, for the composer hastens to his second subject (now in E major), on which he dwells; and still more so with the third one (also in E), which he elaborates with infinite zest. But this gradually dies down, and we end with the "fateful knocks" now almost inaudible, as though dying away in the distance.

[1] The repetition of this section, which Scriabin adopted in his *First Sonata*, has now disappeared with him once for all.

The Finale (*Presto*) which follows is one of the finest movements in the whole range of Scriabin's music. Indeed for completeness of conception and for perfect finish, it would be difficult to find any movement to surpass it in this order. The first theme begins thus :

The subsidiary theme enshrines amongst its delicate filigree work the ubiquitous Fate notes. The first subject then recurs with the addition of a new bass figure of great power and wide sweep. At bar 41 we have the second theme in E flat minor, truly noble in feeling and melodically expressive. It contains wonderful possibilities of development of which the composer is not slow to take advantage. Note the canon at the unison at bars 63 *et seq*. The " Recapitulation " takes place at bar 79, the subsidiary subject being omitted, much importance being attached to the lovely singing melody which appears (still in the minor) over a Dominant Pedal which is developed in a grandiose manner, dying away just before the two unexpected, powerful Tonic chords with which the Sonata terminates.

This Sonata far surpasses the First in unity of thought, in power of expression, and in pure invention. The composer has here thrown off the reflections of the musical giants who preceded him, and has manifested the full individuality of his own brilliant personality.

The Third Sonata, F sharp minor, Opus 23

For the Third Sonata, written in 1897 on the Maidanovoff estate in the Klinsky government, Scriabin uses the form of four-movements. This Sonata was composed almost immediately after the completion of the second one, and it was published by M. P. Belaieff in 1898. The first movement (*Dramatico*, M.M. crotchet=69) appears in regular "Sonata form." The first theme opens with short broken phrases gradually rising in power. There is an impressive nobility about it.[1]

The "second subject" is of a *cantabile* character.

[1] The "pedal" marks here are significant, as this cross-phrasing of the bass accompaniment figure is a feature in all Scriabin's work. The use of the soft pedal in the ninth bar should also be noticed.

The "development," beginning in bar 55 and extending for forty bars, is masterly in every way. It contains a striking augmentation of the second subject, and the commingling of the themes is of great beauty and always of the highest finish.

Unnaturally forced union of subjects was always entirely remote from Scriabin's mind. At the "Recapitulation" (bar 94), the first subject is abbreviated, passing quickly to the second theme in the tonic major. There is a beautiful enharmonic modulation to C major just before the Coda which ends with great power. Note the inner trombone-like passages which give such a richness to Scriabin's pianoforte style. The piece ends softly in the major —another characteristic of his.

The second movement (*Allegretto*) in E flat, commencing *con sordini*, is less individual than the rest of Scriabin's work of this period.

The thick " octave-doubling " at this speed and tone-power is reminiscent of those great yet passing shadows in Schumann's music.

But Schumann was incapable of the heavenly *Trio* portion, which is filled with a purely mystic and unearthly beauty.

A strong counterpoint is then added :

It is simple enough to look at and must be *heard* to be fully appreciated. The thickish subject then returns and affords a wonderful contrast to the middle theme. It becomes more and more animated, and concludes with a triumphant rush on a tonic chord of E flat.

The third movement is an *Andante*[1] in B major. It is metronomed at 63 to the quaver, which many composers would style *poco adagio*. The first theme is full of a heavenly beauty. It breathes of a mystic self-communion in some woodland cloister.

The second theme enters at bar 17. Here the composer deliberately lets go of his tonic moorings. This is well worked over a pedal on D sharp.

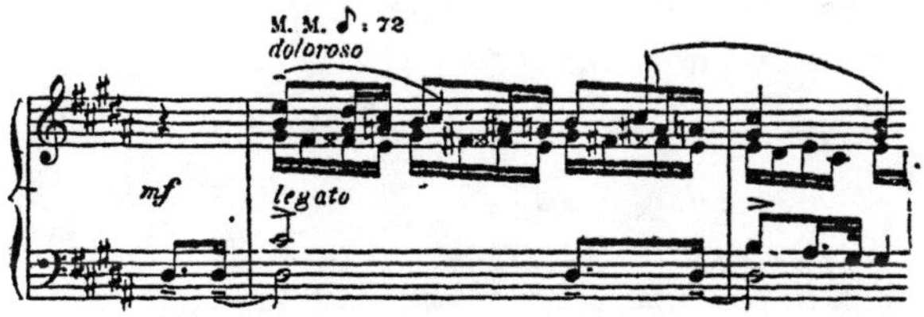

The first theme reappears at bar 33, passing shortly after to the Tenor with elaborate filigree work superimposed. This movement gradually subsides until it passes at bar 50 by a bridge (built on the

[1] See the remark on the *Andante* of the *Pianoforte Concerto*, on page 91.

K

main theme from the opening of the Sonata) straight into the *finale.*

The Finale (*presto con fuoco*) is laid out on modified Sonata-Rondo lines. Notice the chromaticism in the first theme which goes along over a widespread arpeggio bass.

At the seventeenth bar this goes into the bass, and a masterly contrapuntal theme of striking import is added over it. The second subject enters in the relative major at bar 37:

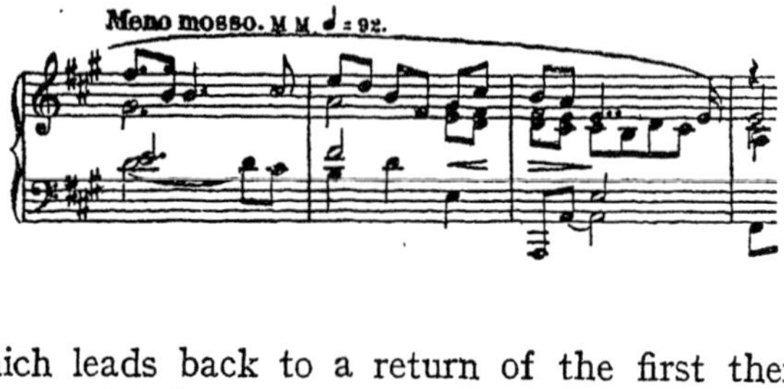

which leads back to a return of the first theme. A powerful development (somewhat frenetic, after the manner of Tchaikovsky) commences at bar 71.

The first theme gathers a longer breath, and opens out into the following extended phrase,

which later appears in the inverted form with a fresh forcible figure added in the bass. Cataclysmic *fugato* entries follow in a veritable tempestuous rioting, on the top of which the first theme (tonic key) comes crowding in before we are aware of it (bar 125), running almost immediately into the "second subject," which now appears in the Tonic major. A second development follows, dying down in nineteen bars over a dominant pedal (C sharp). A *maestoso* Coda enters at bar 202,—one of those hymn-like melodies so dear to the soul of Scriabin. This broadens out and is interspersed with fragments of the first theme, which remains in the bass until the end. The cadence, with its fading references to the first theme, is of uncommon beauty and power, the minor key giving additional strength (not sadness) to the ending.

This Sonata forms the culminating point of Scriabin's first period. Here we have not a suggestion, but the realisation of those characteristics which we shall come to recognise more and more in Scriabin's music as we proceed. Here are his typical melodic curves, his special rhythmic patterns, his characteristic figurations and filigree work—

founded doubtless on Chopinesque lines but carried out with Scriabinistic purity.

Dr. Terry's description of this Sonata is as follows:

> "The first movement opens with an octave figure in the bass, arresting and virile, like a defiant challenge. Scriabin's full grip of every technical resource of the piano is felt, but as far as technical modes of expression are concerned this number resembles MacDowell rather than the Scriabin we come to know later. His interpolation of strong chordal progressions seems to suggest a fine organ extemporisation. We also have the now familiar *duetto* between the two hands, alternating with a single ravishing melody. The first movement subsides quietly on a major chord. The second movement is short; opens and ends turbulently, with an intervening episode of great delicacy. The third movement begins slowly and solemnly in religious mood—yearning, aspiring, contemplation, and restrained ecstasy; this mood swiftly passes, the human begins to stir, we feel the fixed gaze on things of beauty as the 'contemplative' drinks in their sweetness. Later we return to the original rhythmic figure in a rather sinister form. Then comes a tempest-tossed *con fuoco* followed by a heavenly melody; the alternation of these moods bringing the whole to an excellent conclusion."

This Sonata only requires to be more widely known to immediately take its place on the programmes of all our leading pianists. It is remarkable no less for its homogeneity than for its beauty, its great imagination, and its deep expression. A subtle yet close relationship may be traced between the themes of the whole piece. Compare, for instance, the second theme of the first movement as it appears on page 6 with the broadly flowing theme as it is expanded in the first development of the fourth movement (page 21). Psychologically and artistically it is a contribution of the greatest importance to pianoforte literature. Its one defect is Scriabin's whole-hearted devotion to the four-bar phrase, even in his development section ; though it is marvellous that one does not feel this as a detraction from the great beauty of his masterly developments. His pianoforte technique becomes fuller and richer as we pass from one Sonata to another, and although in this Sonata he has not reached the three-stave system, yet he is almost continually securing the effect of three hands on the keyboard.

THE FOURTH SONATA, F SHARP MAJOR, OPUS 30

This work belongs to the transition period of Scriabin's artistic activity. The *Third Sonata* sums up all he could express in the older form. In this *Fourth Sonata*, where he is still working on the older system of harmony, he strives after newer forms. The endeavour to express more and more forceful and definite ideas through the medium of the tonal art is destined to take Scriabin very far along the road, not of reformation, but of veritable innovation.

This Sonata is in two movements, an *Andante*

and a *Prestissimo,* which are not separated, however, but very closely connected in every way. Both are full of happy radiant feeling, and both are cast in the sunny key of F sharp major. The first movement is based on a double theme, and although it is important to remember that Scriabin, like Beethoven, gives no clue more definite than the musical notes themselves as to the real significance of his works, yet it may be helpful here to know that Scriabin described to a friend[1] this bi-partite nature of the theme in the first eight bars thus: the Striving upwards towards the Ideal Creative Power and the motive of resultant Languor or Exhaustion after effort. By this means Scriabin depicts here a number of soul-states in evolution, undergoing, almost from bar to bar, various prismatic spiritual experiences which spring from the one generic idea. Of course, as Eugen Gunst remarks, any attempt to render a definite programme in words or even to class Scriabin as a composer of "programme music," on the lines of Berlioz and others, would be completely foreign to Scriabin's steadfast view of the mission of music. Doubtless all great music is the expression of the feelings rather than of actual events. Henceforth Scriabin has striven in his works to render them more spiritual; but any further attempt to label themes or describe these works in more definite terms of theosophy must be discouraged. Scriabin was content to leave them as music *per se,* and his revelation to Gunst with regard to this

[1] Eugen Gunst: Article on Scriabin's Sonatas in *Soul and Body.*

Sonata, which stands, as it were, at the parting of the ways, may be thankfully accepted as a sign-post merely to show the direction he is going to take in future. It is interesting to observe here that one of our leading English composers, Cyril Scott, admits that Theosophy has helped him very much in his musical composing.

This Fourth Sonata was written in 1903, a period of great creative activity with Scriabin.[1] It was published by Belaieff in 1904.

The two leading motives are announced in a phrase of striking beauty occupying the first eight bars of this beautiful prelude. This may be called " The Striving towards the Ideal " (Ex. *a*), and the " Languor " or " Exhaustion " resulting therefrom (Ex. *b*).

(*a*)[2]

(*b*)

[1] In this summer besides his Sonata he composed about forty more pieces (Op. 30 to Op. 42).

[2] I print it as given, but feel sure the Alto F sharp in bar 1 should be E sharp.

The motives are then developed with the chief stress of the "Languor" motive, which seems to be continually striving to pierce upwards only to fall back again helplessly. The return of the first theme repeated in full, seems to signify the undaunted efforts of the Creative Instinct; and this leads without break into the *Prestissimo volando* (12-8 time) in the same key. This movement is in Sonata-form, the first theme being:

The bridge-subject appears at bar 13, and the "Second Subject" proper at bar 21:

An important feature in the "development" section is the entrance of the "Motive of Desire" from the Prelude, now appearing in full force but in an embittered form:

The fury of this suddenly drops down in the midst of a dominant "pedal-point" to the return of the first theme of the *Presto*, now considerably curtailed, as is also the bridge-portion. The second subject proper is dwelt on at some length, and terminates in a magnificent Coda, the first "leitmotiv" typifying the Ardour of the "Creative Impulse," appearing in its full glory, though now without the "Motive of Languor," as though it has now realised its quest to the full. Gunst says that it is "not the joy of a fully realised desire which is heard, but rather a self-possessed Ecstasy in the Joy of Creation." This is a subtlety into which I cannot enter.

The text of the whole of this Sonata might very well be said to be the Joy of the Exercise of Imaginative Flight liberated from the human trammels. Of course it is spiritualistic in tendency—so is all the best music in the world—and still more so in fineness of harmonic texture; and this piece will rank in the future in this class. In harmonic fineness, invention, and handling of themes, in the majesty and power of the themes themselves, this Sonata represents the highest point reached in this period of Scriabin's creative activity.

FIFTH SONATA, OPUS 53

The *Fifth Sonata* was composed at Lausanne in 1908. It was first published by the author himself at Paris, but was incorporated later in the edition of the Russian Musical Publishing Society.

It was completed in the white fire of inspiration immediately following the orchestral tone-piece *Poem of Ecstasy.*

A quotation from page 11 of the *Poem of Ecstasy* forms the generic idea of the whole of this Sonata. This epigram, which appears in the French and Russian, runs thus:

> " Je vous appelle à la vie, ô forces mystérieuses !
> Noyées dans les obscures profondeurs
> De l'esprit createur, craintives
> Ébauches de vie, à vous j'apporte l'audace."[1]

An introduction of twelve bars rolls back fold by fold, as it were, the curtain of gloom which enwraps the mystery. But we are only yet in the outer region, for a Prologue is then rehearsed with the following for its theme:

This might be styled the Motive of the " Desire for

[1] " I call you to life, O mysterious forces!
Submerged in depths obscure
Of the Creator Spirit, timid embryons of life,
To you I now bring courage."
The Poem of Ecstasy (page 11).

Enlightenment," and bears some relationship to the Desire Motive of the Fourth Sonata. It is developed at some length, and after a bar's silence the movement proper enters (*presto*) in F sharp major (bar 47). This is in regular Sonata form,[1] and the first subject is as follows :

This serves as a summons to the hidden powers. The most striking part of the Sonata occurs at bar 96, a more imperious summons than before, which may be regarded as the second subject.

This challenge is given three times, each time being followed by dim mysterious rumblings as

[1] Scriabin's adherence to the classical form is very remarkable in the face of such tasks of expression as he sets himself. So too is his respect for the four-bar phrase, which amounts to an obsession.

of some strange and distant cosmic system. An additional call of considerable majesty is added.

As a third subject we have a lyrical utterance of great beauty softly breathed through soothing harmonies. Gunst fancifully explains this as the cosmic world called to embryonic life.

But a strange interruption now occurs.

Things seem to take an unexpected cosmic turn. The curtain of gloom again obscures everything. It is rolled aside afresh, and the themes are still further developed. Almost every available key and colour is used to throw more light on the themes in this development portion which extends from bar 157 to bar 329. In many passages—notably in bars 273–274, and again at 277–278—his great masterpiece, *Prometheus: the Poem of Fire*, is foreshadowed.

Before we leave the development section, the transformed appearance of the lyric (third) subject with its bold chromatic counterpoint should be noticed (page 14, last stave).

The sheer ecstasy of this is suddenly changed to the appearance of the "first subject" proper (now in B major) which heralds in the Return section.

Here the three chief evocatory subjects are again unrolled with increased power, only to be answered by the *Allegro* of the powers of darkness who now menace and with a weird intoxication, vertiginous with fury (according to the indications), but powerfully driven back by a luminous motive of blinding light (see next page), which pierces its way through as it were to a glorious vision of Light and Life. The motive of the Prologue here appears in its most resplendent light; it is set out on a three-stave arrangement which taxes the powers of the player to the uttermost.

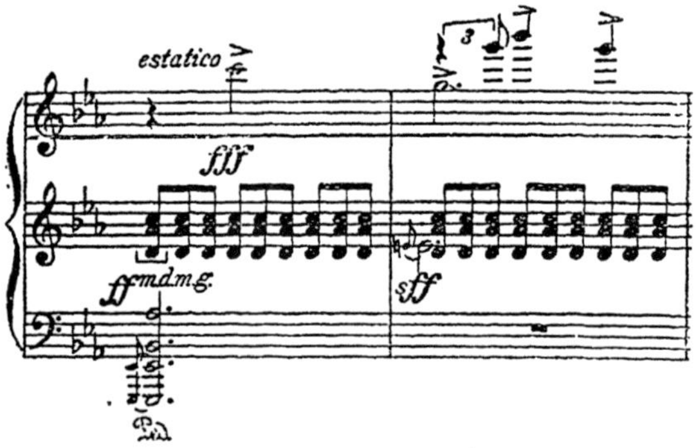

But the glimpse of radiant light is only, as it were, momentary, the mutterings recurring in a *Presto* Coda; and despite the sudden call for the Light again, with a thunderclap and a lightning flash the curtain of Obscurity is quickly dropped —the vision vanishes—a deep silence reigns over all. . . .

Technically this Sonata is of extreme interest. Whilst the harmonic innovations extend to formation as advanced as those used in his *Prometheus*, he here achieves them along the old lines. Henceforward he drops the key-signature altogether.[1] His growing fondness for the use of chords built up by 4ths is also apparent. For lyrical counterpoint of exquisite beauty, the third *meno-vivo* theme is peerless.

[1] This is not the same thing as saying that he abandons his Tonic (like the Post-Impressionists), but merely that he hesitates to use a signature involving the use of sharps and flats at the same time. For a further inquiry into the problem of mixed key-signatures, see the author's *Modern Harmony: its Explanation and Application* (Augener), Chapter VI, page 70.

As regards the technique of piano-playing a great move forward has here been made. The work increases in difficulty, but with Scriabin one can never say that his work is "un-pianistic."[1]

His wonderful mastery of light and shade (chiaroscuro) renders this work a complete masterpiece, for it ranges quite freely over the full extent of the keyboard. The sonority of tone obtained and the rich radiant display of the ecstatic "Glimpse of the Pure Light" in the Coda (page 19) is a masterpiece of handling of pianoforte technique.

Whilst we have here drawn somewhat freely on the psychological, or should we say theosophical, explanation of this Sonata, following Gunst's outlines, which he received from the composer himself, sufficient stress cannot be laid on the fact that Scriabin was quite content to leave the Sonata to speak for itself, with only the little stanza of four lines to point the way to the new territory which the composer felt he was entering. Such a reserve is justifiable.

As an illustration, we may take the description of this Sonata by Dr. Terry, who obviously did not know Gunst's explanation of it.

> "It opens impetuously, soon sinking into tranquillity and contemplation. The melodies are now more aloof and disembodied. After

[1] I am not at all sure of a contrary charge that the application of his new harmonic system in his later orchestral works is far too "pianistic" and not sufficiently orchestral in principle.

another impetuous outburst it subsides once more, and above a rich and warm accompaniment wrings the heart with the torture of a bitter-sweet melody. A rude interruption, like a sharp stab, gives place to the sweet pain of the previous melodic figure; suppressed agitation as of uneasy heaving under a heavy load, shouldered gladly at length with triumphant effort. Two themes—sinister and mystical—later seem to war with each other till one is tossed on a sea of passion which at last dies down, and the sonata ends on the familiar contemplative note—serene, content, and tranquil. To my mind (at present at any rate) this is the finest of the sonatas."

I myself played it for many years with some similar emotional scheme in my mind.

As a *tour-de-force* in composition, whilst the creation of the *Second Sonata* was spread over a period of five years, Scriabin in the full mastery which he had already obtained in the new medium conceived and completed the whole of this Sonata in the amazingly short time of three or four days.

The Sixth Sonata, Opus 62

In his *Sixth Sonata* Scriabin has definitely entered the new region of harmony, from which he never in future looked back for one instant. In his restless search for an ever more refined and perfected medium, for a more and more highly concentrated spiritual expression, we have continually found him hitherto straining at the bonds of the older technique—breaking out first one place and then another into new regions. And now with this Sonata all the old landmarks have disappeared—even the key-signature is abandoned.[1]

The harmonic question has been fully discussed in Chapter IX. Suffice to say here that, for his proper expression in this deeply mystic Sonata, Scriabin finds the following ground-chord necessary: "G, C sharp, F, B, E, and A flat."

The chord in the treble stave is doubled in the octave above, the full combination being played by a double revolution of overlapping hands. This Sonata was completed whilst the composer was at Beattenberg (Switzerland) in 1911. The *Sixth, Seventh,* and *Ninth Sonatas* were probably all sketched out there during the spring. The *Sixth Sonata* was published by the Russian Musical Publishing Society in 1912.

We cannot repeat too often that Scriabin's music is not of the Programme order (as with Liszt, Berlioz, and Strauss). Everyone must put their own interpretation of these wonderfully suggestive pieces. For those who may be appalled by the very strangeness of this new music, here is a sort of story I fitted to it on first hearing it. I might fancy something altogether different on hearing it again at some other time.

[1] But the Sonata has still a firm hold on tonality. It may justly be said to be in the key of G, for the Tonic has not gone but merely the Dominant. See the author's *Modern Harmony: its Explanation and Application* (Chapter IV, on the Duodecuple Scale).

I see in this Sonata then a Russian version (in pure music) of the idea which inspired the Englishman Newman's *Dream of Gerontius.*

The first subject, the THEME OF THE SOUL, is full of that feeling of strange flight, "that inexpressive lightness," and that "sense of freedom never felt before," of which Newman speaks.

The bridge begins at bar 15. With the second subject the dream takes more definite shape.

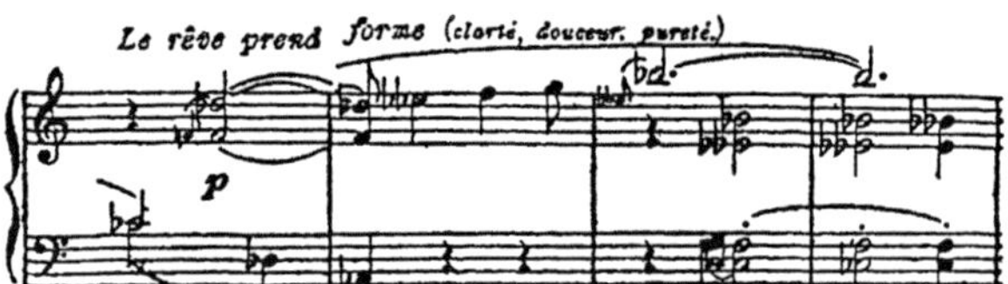

Here again a quotation of Newman is appropriate.

> "This silence pours a solitariness
> Into the very essence of my soul;
> And the deep rest, so soothing and so sweet,
> Hath something too of sternness and of pain."

The pristine purity of this is suddenly embittered, however, by a small but disquieting counterpoint of two notes which first enters in bar 56, remaining permanently with the theme.

Some crowding figures suggestive of flight

bring strange forebodings of terror into the third subject :

which rises into a fierce hubbub, culminating in veritable demoniacal howls of dissonance at the idea that humans should

> " . . . Aspire
> To become gods by a new birth."

A confusion of all the former themes follows in this development portion, and the motives of flight are almost continuous. The second part of the first subject is marshalled with increasing strength of formation. A mysterious call is continually heard.

A Miltonic struggle between the forces of good and evil is in progress—a time of trial and testing.

The powers of evil are dispersed and the " Soul Theme " emerges with a tender radiance.

The return section now enters (page 13, last stave, bar 2). The second subject proper is omitted, but a remarkable view of the " Ego Theme " takes its place on a three-stave arrangement. The upward soaring soul is broadly spread on the upper, whilst diminished forms of this soaring theme are continually being heard in the bass. See bars 244 *et seq.* (pages 16 and 17). This is given twice, but on the following page (18) we have a still more widely spread arrangement, for a tenor canon is added. It is doubtful if greater demands on the ten figures have ever been made in the whole range of pianoforte literature; a second player for these passages would add greatly to their fluency and clearness.

But the hosts of evil now return with redoubled force; terror seizes hold of the soul, which passes disillusioned through a period of dismay and terror and becomes at length absorbed in the dizzy delicious dance of the Joy-molecules of the cosmic world. This palpitating, whirling dance forms the Coda[1] to this remarkable piece.

Newman in his poem allows the soul to find peace and purity. Scriabin, on the other hand, seems to leave the powers of evil rampant, and the soul still struggling.

The Seventh Sonata, Opus 64

This Sonata was also written in Beattenberg in 1911, and indeed was finished before the Sixth. In this composition the thickened mystic atmosphere reaches its zenith. Of the two opposing forces, the one is still more brutal, whilst the other is even more refined and tender. The first theme appears thus :

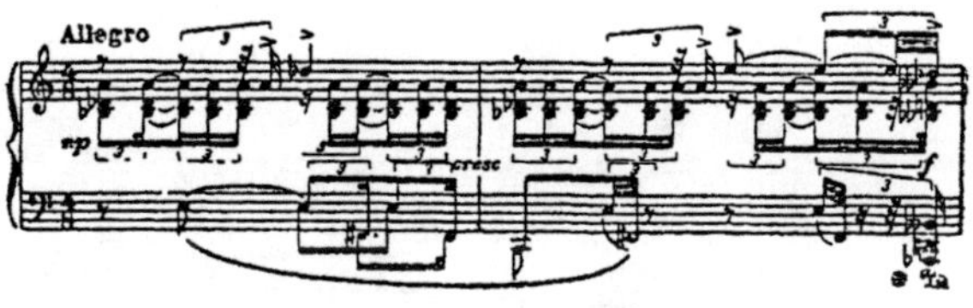

A second theme enters in the horn register :

[1] Scriabin's *technique* here approaches somewhat closely in appearance to Schönberg's method. But Scriabin has a logic which the Austrian has not.

The mysterious bell-figure which occurs at the end of the second part of the first subject (first appearing at bar 26) becomes an important feature throughout the Sonata.

The " second subject " proper, marked " with a heavenly happiness," appears at bar 29.

Notice the counterpoint which accompanies it: C𝄪, A sharp, and A natural;[1] as this receives a special development in the Coda (bars 297 *et seq.*). The second subject has also another important counterpoint which first appears at bar 39.

In the conclusion of the " Exposition " considerable combination and development of themes takes place; and there is also a most striking harmonic

[1] These notes are " ringed " in the musical illustration.

passage which sounds like a discordant tolling from some nether-world.

This codetta runs into the " Development proper " at bar 92 (page 8, stave 1, bar 1). This is of considerable length; the second subject proper passing through many transmutations. The music here is of exceeding picturesqueness, the passing of the themes being mingled with the tolling of innumerable deep-toned bells, and with terrifying outbursts of distant thunder-claps.

The second theme notably goes through many transmutations. This development portion ends with two remarkable " pedal-points "—one on E, the other on the lowest C sharp.

The Recapitulation section is surprisingly regular, except for the amazing harmony of the now fierce first theme, and the piling up of counterpoints, big with import, on to the second subject proper. These are shaken off one by one until (on page 18) the theme appears in the comparatively simple but charming harmonic sheen of the " Dominant ninth " (page 18). The Scriabinic Coda[1] is no less remarkable for its extent than for its contents. A vertiginous

[1] Of a kind vaguely hinted at in some of Mahler's Symphonies and only once partially achieved by Debussy in his scintillating " Fêtes."

dance of unrestrained joy carries a new melody, founded, however, on the first counterpoint to the second subject, which bounds along with it in its headlong course to a climax on one of the most remarkable chords ever written. Three mysterious tolls are heard, and the sounds fly away into thin air.

THE EIGHTH SONATA, OPUS 66

The *Eighth Sonata* was written at Moscow in the first half of 1913. It was published by P. Jurgenson in the same year. In extent and scope it is the longest of all the Sonatas—thirty-one pages long—and moreover it is written all in one movement.

In this Sonata, as in all the other works, Scriabin intended the music to speak for itself. Such directions as are given in the French indications are only for the assistance of the player and not for the listener.

The Sonata is founded on the following remarkable sequence of chords, which constitute its first motive.

The " foundation chord " of the whole piece is the second one, marked (*a*), not the *first one,* as Gunst states.

The *Lento* Prologue contains besides two other motives the following sinuous theme on the middle stave, and the figure of flight in the fourth bar of the upper stave.

The Prologue extends for twenty-one bars. We come then to the Sonata form proper (bar 22):

with the following pendant:

A considerable amount of development follows before the second subject proper makes its appearance:

This second theme has also a pendant. The codetta

which follows reintroduces the motives of the Prologue.

A development follows of Brobdingnagian proportions—nearly two hundred bars. The following figure should be noticed :

The "Recapitulation" section comes round at bar 329. This is not shortened, but extended. The Coda over a Tonic pedal is of remarkable harmonic daring, ending with a characteristic atomic *Prestissimo,* a cosmic dance which vibrates untiringly, and finally gradually vanishes into space.

The Ninth Sonata, Opus 68

Although this Sonata was completed in Moscow in 1913, it dates from the period of the *Sixth* and *Seventh Sonatas,* when the composer was at Beattenberg. It is only about half the length of the *Eighth,* and is more poetic and idealistic both in form and texture. It commences *moderato quasi andante,* and becomes gradually faster and faster from the middle onwards to the Coda, which is a veritable dance of joy. This fades away, however, towards the end, into the remote atmosphere of the opening bars.

For the opening, Scriabin follows his favourite plan of first creating a harmonic veil through which the first chief subject may shine clearly (bar 5) :

There is a pendant to it—a mysterious murmuring subject, low-pitched :

Later on the movement proper enters with the following theme :

followed by a "second subject" of languorous nature.

The musical atmosphere breathes of a pure radiant crepuscular reverie, and here, as in many other cases, one feels the music to be allied distantly to the poetic naturalism of Debussy.[1]

This second subject is in reality the chief theme of the Sonata. The development portion begins at the 69th bar (page 6, stave 4), which brings about a gradual disillusionment of the reverie, an effect produced chiefly by harmonic aberrations.

The "Recapitulation" portion begins in bar 155. In the 179th bar the second theme loses its

[1] As displayed for instance in his *Prelude, L'après-midi d'un faune.*

original purity, becoming distorted almost beyond recognition. A queer little marching passage emphasises this.

The theme spends itself out gradually in a characteristic Scriabinic dance of cosmic atoms, mounting with ever-increasing palpitation into a veritable molecular vertigo. The mist of the nightmare dispels—the painful memories fly away—leaving the pure semi-luminosity of the atmosphere of the opening bars.

The Tenth Sonata, Opus 70

This Sonata was written in Moscow in 1913. In contrast to the preceding one we have here a kind of crepuscular twilight. It is a pianoforte[1] counterpart of the orchestral *Prometheus*—a radiant

[1] Or rather "fortepiano" as the Russians call it, in print. But in general parlance the grand piano is called a "royale" and the upright a "pianino"; so polyglottic are their technical terms.

poem of pure vibrant sunlight throughout. The Prologue contains the following motives :

(*a*)

(*b*)

The main Sonata-like movement enters in the thirty-ninth bar with the *Allegro* :

The second subject enters at bar 73 (page 5, stave 1), and as in the preceding Sonata really forms the chief theme of the work.

It has a striking pendant (bars 84–87) :

After this the exposition is completed in a further twenty-seven bars ; the development portion proper commencing at bar 115 with the "*a*" motive of the Prologue. This "working-out" section is very remarkable,

and reaches its culmination in the "*Puissant, radieux*" presentation of the second subject—the Soul Theme (bar 212, page 11). The harmonic technique is here very striking. This powerful scintillating passage looks like a piece of Ornstein transposed to the top of the keyboard.

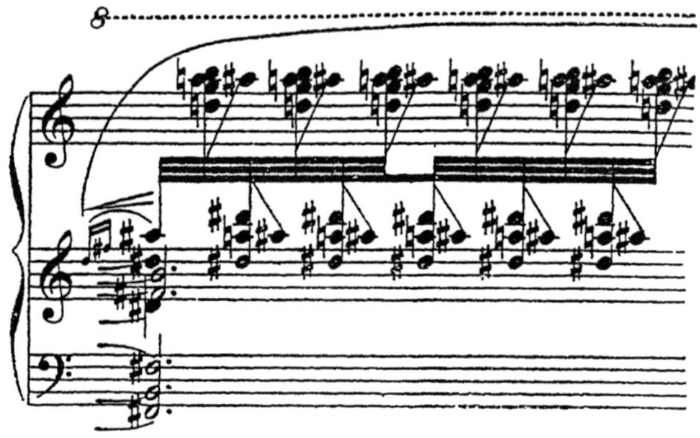

Two bars (222 and 223) connect it with the "Recapitulation" section, the "first subject" proper entering at the *Allegro*. The second subject appears here transposed a major third lower, more luminously and brilliantly accompanied. The curious little harmonic pendant still remains, and the whole piece is consummated in one of those stirring vibrating atomic dances of accumulating velocity with which Scriabin has concluded the *Eighth* and *Ninth Sonatas*.

The Prologue themes are then used as an Epilogue, and the piece closes with a rather conventional Plagal cadential form, which, however, reinforces unusual upper harmonic tones, and has a curious little bell-figure of three notes added :

The emotional-colour scheme works out something like this. The dreamer lies on the hillside in that dim mysterious twilight which precedes sunrise on the mountain-tops. The veil of mist gradually disappears. Things become more defined and vibrant. The first subject (*allegro*) enters with some vague, inchoate emotion—the pulse gently stirring and warming until finally the Ego Theme (the second subject) comes to full birth. Ravishment, tenderness, joy, warmth, and colour, and all which spring from the sun, increase with the growth of the Ego. More and more vibrant everything grows until the Ego Theme appears to have become part of the sun-rays themselves—purified by fire, itself a Sun, dancing the cosmic dance of the Coda, —a veritable palpitating Pæan of scintillating molecules. . . . Finally, the dream becomes paler, and gradually passes away into the thin ether across which sound cannot travel, but only light. The dreamer awakes and finds himself on the cold hillside—still in the crepuscular light of the Prologue, the music of which is again used as Epilogue.

It is noteworthy that the last two Sonatas show at times a turn to a less involved harmonic texture.

We have dwelt at even more considerable length on the Pianoforte Sonatas than on the Orchestral Symphonies of Scriabin, as in them the gradual evolution of his genius can be more clearly traced. In order to make the view of these periods clearer and better balanced, the last four Sonatas must be regarded as one phase, as they were conceived almost simultaneously during his visit to Beattenberg in 1911.

Having regard to the sketches for his proposed *Mystery*, Scriabin seems to have passed away somewhat from this musico-theosophic stage, into one more concerned with a combination of the mystery of light, colour, and movement, and their unification into one new definite art. Herein I think he was striving at an unattainable, even undesirable goal. Like Wagner with his so-called " new art-drama " and like Columbus too, he set out to find a musical " Eldorado "—and discovered a new continent instead. I do not think he has established any definite union between Theosophy and Music, but he has immensely widened the possibilities of the purely tonal art.

In the wonderfully picturesque Dante-like imagination of the *Fifth Sonata ;* in the romance of the *Sixth ;* in the portrayal of the elemental world-forces in the Seventh; the crystalline transparency of the Eighth; the weird and sinister terrors of the Ninth, and finally in the radiant Tenth, we have a contribution to instrumental music of the greatest importance perhaps since Beethoven.

XI

THE FIVE SYMPHONIES

SCRIABIN wrote five Symphonies; using the term in its broadest sense to include the three last orchestral works which some would call Tone-Poems. They run thus: First (Choral) Symphony in E, Second Symphony in C, Third Symphony (*The Divine Poem*), Fourth the *Poem of Ecstasy*, and Fifth the *Prometheus*. There was also an early orchestral *Reverie* (a juvenile work) and a Pianoforte Concerto (Op. 3), and at the time of his death he was engaged on his projected greatest masterpiece, *Mystery*.

But this is by no means the order in which we have become acquainted with Scriabin's orchestral works. The following table gives the few isolated performances which have come westwards:

London Performances:—

Mar. 13, 1913. *First Symphony*. Royal Philharmonic Society.
(Conductor, Safonoff.)

Feb. 2, 1913. *Prometheus*. Queen's Hall.
(Conductor, Sir Henry J. Wood.)
(Pianist, Mr. Arthur Cooke.)

Oct. 18, 1913. *Third Symphony*. Queen's Hall.
(Conductor, Sir Henry J. Wood.)

March 14, 1914. *Prometheus*. Queen's Hall.
(Conductor, Sir Henry J. Wood.)
(Pianist, Scriabin.)

New York Performances:—

Andante from First Symphony (1913).
Prometheus with Colours (1914).

These performances were given promiscuously without relation to one another; and, with one exception (the *Third Symphony*), the works were only partially given, and nearly always were shorn of some important accessories. In the case of the tardy English performances of the *First Symphony*, five movements only were given, the last three choral movements being omitted; and the English performances of *Prometheus* have hitherto lacked the element of colour as well as the choral parts. The two Symphonies were played to entirely different audiences. The American cautiousness in approaching this Russian composer is worthy of note. In England, Safonoff only was entirely responsible for beginning at the right end with the *First Symphony*, a beautiful melodious work which he gave in London, Liverpool, and other places; but always (probably on account of practicable difficulties) *minus* its Choral Epilogue. The main object of the London *Prometheus* performances seems to have been the mere satisfaction of that eager but rather shallow curiosity in ultra-modernity in art which characterised that Spring season of 1914 which immediately preceded the great European War.

What would have been the fate of Beethoven's

works in England had we been introduced in the first instance to the *Ninth Symphony* and the later quartets, with no other preparation than perhaps the knowledge of a few of the undistinctive works of a precocious childhood which had filtered through into private drawing-rooms, and nothing more?

Yet this is exactly the way Scriabin has been forced on us. A few of his little pieces, Opp. 1, 2, and 3, perhaps even the early set of Preludes (Op. 11), had percolated into England, when suddenly we were faced with his most extreme orchestral work. Some compunction was evidently felt as to the ability of the audience to understand so complicated and novel a piece of music; but surely some less brutal policy than the plan of playing the work twice at one Concert could have been found. Who would want to hear, say, the *Ninth Symphony* of Beethoven through twice running? Even the players, excellent as they were, were thought by the brilliant Russian critic, Briantchaninoff, not to have realised fully the proper feeling of the work.

This inverse method of becoming acquainted with an artist's works was only a repetition of what happened to Tchaikovsky. But Tchaikovsky (like Bach) was one of those composers who attain the full zenith of their powers almost at the first bound; and though they reap the benefit of their ripe technique for a long time, they never step beyond their high-water mark so early achieved. Such a plan was by no means detrimental—rather perhaps advantageous to Tchaikovsky; but it was the reverse with Scriabin.

In no other composer is the steady onward progression in his art more remarkable. With him the evolutionary process is perfectly clear, for he advances a definite step in technique and expression with each successive work. Whether we take the first set of Sonatas, or the Preludes and Études, or the Symphonies alone, this rise in the evolutionary scale can be plainly seen. Is it not then of the first importance that these works should be heard in historical order, if they are to be properly understood?

The first two Symphonies belong to his early but yet mature period. The Third marks the Transition stage into the theosophic region. It expresses the liberation of the spirit from temporal fetters, the self-affirmation of personality. The Fourth expresses the composer's Ecstasy of untrammelled action, his Joy in Creative Activity, and the Fifth (*Prometheus*) the real Life of the Spirit in its ceaseless rising efforts towards the fuller light of knowledge. In the latter, Scriabin uses a new medium more suited to his purpose. His "mystic chord" introduces into music a new system of harmony constructed on intervals of the Fourth.

First Symphony

Lento in E major, 3–4 *time.*
Allegro dramatico in E minor, 3–4 *time.*
Lento in B major, 6–8 *time.*
Vivace in C major, 9–8 *time.*
Allegro in E minor, 3–4 *time.*
Andante in E major, 3–4 *time.* (Two Solo Voices.)
Choral Finale in E (with Fugue in C).

The *First Symphony* was written in the composer's eighteenth and nineteenth years, when he was finishing his courses at the Moscow Conservatoire. It is a work revealing the most precocious talents as a composer, and it is a matter of continual wonderment to me that after such a work his quondam tutor Arensky should have continued to "see no reason why the young man should devote himself to the career of a musical composer."

The plan of the work is laid out on the broadest possible lines. The early use of an Epilogue and Prologue is noteworthy. The Symphony form proper is revealed in movements II to V. The *Lento* commences with the following Clarinet theme :

Then comes the following finely coloured theme :

The second movement, *Allegro dramatico*, is in the

usual symphonic Sonata form. The first subject has a fine " stringy " feeling :

The second subject is also in dark colours, and the melody on the low clarinet notes has a charming appeal.

The clarinet also figures prominently in the third movement, *Lento;* the first subject being a sweet expressive melody in the medium register.

The second subject goes on to the Wood-wind in the approved Tchaikovskian manner with little fluttering couplets of chromatics on the strings.

Reminiscences of Tchaikovsky's *Sixth Symphony*

creep again into the fourth movement, *Vivace,* a palpitating highly coloured piece, opening thus :

The second subject is striking on account of its *faerie* treatment :

The fifth movement *Allegro* falls back to some solid string work. The first subject being thickened out by strings, clarinet, and bassoons in Unison.

The second subject is the weakest in the whole Symphony. This movement also is laid out on "Sonata" lines.

Two solo voices, *Mezzo Soprano* and *Tenor,* are introduced in the sixth movement, a "Hymn of

Art," the subject matter of which is drawn from the Prologue. The Voices sing :

> "*Pure symbol of the Living God,*
> *Sublimest art of Harmony,*
> *We raise our fervent hearts to thee*
> *In wonder at your melody.*"

Later on the chorus enters with some effective antiphony, leading into the final Choral Fugue. Truly a striking work for one not yet twenty years of age. The movements are straightforward and uninvolved. Somewhat unexpectedly in these precocious talents we find, if anything, too strict an adherence, almost too reverent an attitude, towards form and construction—a very good fault at any rate in the early years. Shadows of Tchaikovsky, of Dvorak, of Weber, and Wagner fly across the music constantly, but there is plenty of individuality already forthcoming, and the masterly handling of the orchestra is full of promise for the rich things in store. The Prologue is a well-finished piece ; but it is easy to point to weak places elsewhere. Some of the "bridge work" proclaims the juvenile mind. There is a naïve little touch at the end of the development of the second movement when he marks his horns *pavillon en l'air*. The Fugue also smacks of the schoolroom. Indeed it is a regular "school fugue" on a very ordinary subject; but the whole conception is sufficiently broad to proclaim the advent of a great master of form, style, and expression. There is a superfluity of perfect cadences, but there is also an effort to unify the whole work, notably by the return of the Prologue themes at the sixth movement.

One of the great charms of the work is the wealth of wonderful singing passages which he gives to his orchestral basses. On the other hand, the choral work is elementary. Voices never appealed greatly to Scriabin, and Modern Choralism, as we understand it, is unknown in Russia. It is interesting, however, to compare the choral part here with that in *Prometheus*, the only other occasion on which he wrote for voices, either Choral or Solo.

The Full Score of this Symphony was published by Belaieff in 1900. There is an arrangement for Piano Duet (four hands) by A. Winkler.

The Second Symphony in C major, Opus 29

Andante in C minor, 4–4 time.
Allegro, E flat, 6–8 time.
Andante, B major, 6–8 time.
Tempestuoso, F minor, 12–8 time; leading into
Finale: Maestoso, C major, 4–4 time.

This is an even larger creation than the *First Symphony*, and dates from the period of his tutorial work at the Moscow Conservatoire (from 1897 to 1903). Indeed it was almost the only work of importance written during these six "lean years." It is in five movements, the first—an *Andante* Prologue—supplying the material for the fifth—the Epilogue. The largest movements are the three middle ones, an *Allegro*, E flat, 6–8 time; an *Andante* (metronomed at 44), B major; and a *Tempestuoso*, F minor, 12–8, leading into the Epilogue.

The Symphony is not scored for an extravagant orchestra; 3 Flutes, 2 Oboes, 3 Clarinets, 2 Bassoons, 4 Horns, 3 Trumpets, 3 Trombones, and Tuba, Drums, and the usual Strings. The first subject of the opening *Andante* is immediately given out on a solo Clarinet.

This theme is of considerable importance, and it is metamorphosed to form the first subject of the *Finale.* Both the handling and the development are a great step onwards from the *First Symphony.* The second subject is given to a Solo Violin in order to impart a more etherealised colour to it.

This subject also is used again in the Epilogue. A long development follows, and on the first subject emerging more clearly—triumphantly, the movement passes over without break to the *Allegro* Return. The first subject goes bounding along on the strings with graceful ease :

and the Clarinet (a much favoured instrument with

Scriabin as with many others) again claims the second subject.

The harmony of this is significantly predicative in places of the composer's later obsession for chords built up by fourths (see Chapter IX). The movement follows the usual mode of development, working up to a fine climax before the Recapitulation. A powerful aspiring melody appears in the Coda in the brass instruments.

It is accompanied by swirling chromatic counterpoints on the strings. Already the young composer has a Wagnerian mastery of orchestral handling and colour. It is somewhat surprising to find the third movement marked *Andante,* yet metronomed at 44 to the crotchet. The Italian term really means "going" or "walking," but we must remember that the Russian—even the soldier on the march—walks very slowly; he makes up for it in impetuosity and speed in the fast movements. This *Andante* in B is a delightful *Pastorale,* full of lovely singing melodies, sometimes given to a solo violin, sometimes to a cello, and occasionally to the full violins with rich cello counter-melodies; all in a happy summer mood, occasionally amorously inclined. The composer must have been possessed of a deep content when he penned this delightful movement, page after page filled with the warbling of birds, the ripple of rivulets, and the whisper of the shady trees, and the happiness of the country under a summer sun. Marvellous to relate, it is in perfect "Sonata form"—a form always regarded by Beethoven and Mozart as far too long for such slow movements. The second subject reminds one of Elgar's *Second Symphony*.

The fourth movement is a tempestuous *Allegro* in F minor, with broad windy sweeps of melody and shuddering string passages.

Some fine bold counterpoint enters later on:

The second romantic subject, tinged with a slight melancholy,

is very short-lived, being engulfed in a veritable tempest which breaks out, carrying everything before its swirling torrents. The theme of the Prologue is heard amongst the tempest on the horns; so too is the first subject of the *Allegro*, but the riotous mood persists, rising to climax after climax, until a broadly laid-out bridge (also borrowed from the Prologue) leads into the Finale. This opens with a pompous theme evolved from the first clarinet melody of the Prologue.

A Wagnerian sequence of forceful brass chords leads to a tender second subject given out on the flute. The first subject then returns, still more magnificently arrayed. The second subject now broadens out, however, more and more, until it has achieved its full magnificence, when a long "Dominant pedal-point" ushers in the Recapitulation of the Exposition of the Finale in full, the principal subject of the *Allegro* (second movement) appearing together with the *Pomposo* one in the Coda.

This Symphony is a distinct advance on the first one. The subjects are (with few exceptions) very striking; the orchestra is deftly handled, and there is a broad homogeneity in the planning as well as in the combining of the themes and movements. The unwise adoption of the full "Sonata form" for so many of the movements protracts the Symphony unduly. This is especially the case with the slow movement, which is much too long. The last two movements do not achieve the high distinction of the others. The *Pomposo* theme evolved from the charming clarinet melody of the opening appears tawdry in the magniloquence of the major key. The Symphony contains many unnecessary bridges —mere scholastic ones at that. Two of these have a curiously old-fashioned diatonic formula:

In fact the number of Dominant pedals is a serious blemish on the Symphony. Moreover, they are uncalled-for and could easily be "cut" in performance. The full "Recapitulation" of all these Sonata movements is a pity, as the construction of the Symphony as a whole is remarkably good in other ways, and the themes are of great beauty and originality. The fine quality of the singing melodies on the basses is noteworthy; so is the contrapuntal juxtaposition of many of the themes, and there are passages and climaxes of immense grandeur and power.

Much as I am opposed to "cuts" I think there is every excuse for them in this Symphony. They could be done without interfering in any way with the "programme" which one feels to be at the basis of this fine work. Would not the composer prefer a performance "with cuts" rather than no performance at all? The many beauties of the work are too good to be relegated to limbo. The *Andante* makes a fine excerpt.

The Full Score was published by Belaieff in 1903. A very effective arrangement of the work for piano duet has been made by B. Kalafaty.

THE THIRD SYMPHONY ("THE DIVINE POEM") IN C MINOR AND MAJOR, OPUS 43

The Third Symphony (*The Divine Poem*) has been explained as the expression of the liberation of the life of the spirit from its temporal fetters—the affirmation of personality. It was written in the most fruitful season of all Scriabin's creative work—the summer of 1903—when probably he himself especially felt the joys of a free creative life as compared with the humdrum routine of tutorial work. He must indeed have felt "wings to his spirit," and the creations of this period are characterised by imaginative flights of unusual loftiness, whilst his work is permeated with the optimistic feeling of a great abiding happiness.

This Symphony is laid out on the following lines:

Lento in C minor, 3–2 time (Prologue).
Allegro in C minor, 3–4 ("Strife").
Lento in E major, 3–4 ("Sensuous Pleasures").
Allegro in C major ("Divine Activity").

The first three bars of the short but magnificent Prologue (sixteen bars) give the three "leading motives" of the Symphony: "Divine Grandeur," "The Summons to Man," and the "Fear to approach, suggestive of Flight."

(*a*)

(*b*)

(c)

These are combined throughout the work with the various subjects, and indeed some of the subjects are derived directly from them.

The *Allegro* ("Strife") is marked "Mysterious, Tragic." The first subject with a fine leaping grace is given to the violins, and is sixteen bars in length.

Then comes the first suggestion of divinity in connection with it.

This theme becomes more and more confident as we proceed. When it dares to appear a little bolder,

it does so only with a watchful care, and with the first subject (Human Personality) in the Bass below it. The soaring of the spirit becomes more daring with

but the upward aspiring curves gradually become more feeble and attenuated

as they fall down to the second subject proper:

Curiously enough this belongs to the same spiritual plane as many of Elgar's themes.

A mood of lassitude passes over the music, and with the third subject (or is it the "second subject proper"? It matters little):

we are in an even more unworldly atmosphere—*romantique, légendaire.* A triumphal passage of majestic harmony[1]

brings in the return of the Divine Theme with great power.

This completes the exposition (about 270 bars), and is followed by a lengthy development and a full Recapitulation section. The development begins with the first subject *mistico,* which soon mounts in force, only to be cut across by a scale figure of considerable power and extent. The aspiring theme of the brass harmony (see above) enters, but only leads to a formidable crashing overthrow. (There is a Wagnerian touch about the chromatic scales in the violins here.) The rallying call becomes more imperative, and a solid climax is accordingly built up triumphantly. We pass once more into the legendary atmosphere. A new theme is born, tender and wrapped in feelings of transport, a theme destined for the chief subject of the slow movement, then the Divine Theme reappears, but still followed by motives of Fear and Flight. This brings us to the Recapitulation section when every subject reappears in full, except for the first few bars of the

[1] Note the Bass progression by major 3rds. See page 186.

second subject (No. 3, page 181). There is a Coda of wild, precipitant flight:

and the Divine Theme returns in blazing splendour with a significant counter subject.

A short bridge leads us straight into the *Lento* ("Voluptes"), metronomed at 50 to the crotchet. These pleasures are very solemn ones. Now we see why the second subject of the first movement was omitted in its recapitulatory section, for the chief subject of this slow movement appears to have a close affinity to it.

A chromatic episode succeeds this, marked "*avec une ivresse débordante,*" crossed by a new crashing motive, which gives way in turn to a restful passage completely diatonic with limpid arpeggios. This very gradually hushes down to a whispering lulling which is almost silence itself, over which the chief subject (see above, *Lento*) of the movement appears long drawn out by a solo violin *dolcissimo*. There is some exceedingly beautiful harmony here :

Voluptuous and passionate phrases follow, continually increasing in power, until we reach the motive of Divine Aspiration, wildly crossed by the crashing motive :

which leads into the last movement (*Allegro*), Divine Activities. The opening subject is comprised of the two little motives, one taken from the Prologue, the other from the theme of " Joyful Soaring." It is marked " with radiant joy."

A short breathless entry of the bridge-subject of the first movement appears, calming down into a new melody—the second subject proper of this movement.

This, the so-called EGO Theme, is destined for great things, for it symbolises the translation of human personality into celestial regions. A sweet limpid melody then enters :

after which the EGO melody expands and blossoms out into this glorious creation.

The subjects are all fully treated again in the Recapitulation, and the work is consummated with one of the finest perorations in the whole range of music. As a sheer effort of the imagination, the Symphony is an immense achievement ; the themes are magnificent ; the handling of counterpoint and form is masterly in the extreme; the harmony wonderfully coloured, always of a rich sonority in soft passages as well as in loud. The cohesion, combination, development, and even, one might say, the birth of the themes (the way they gradually emerge) is most noteworthy. The harmony affords a study in itself. One particular formula of major 3rds in the Bass—for instance, C, A flat, E, C, G sharp—is much affected by Bantock. (See the music example given on page 182.) The rich singing basses of his first two Symphonies are still in pleasing evidence. But I have two faults to find with the work. Is the Symphony any better for such a Programme? I doubt it. The outlined programme is of course unavoidable in view of the very full directions in French which are inserted in the score, but in my mind such a programme or explanation is altogether superfluous. The message of the music—magnificent as it is—is not so extraordinary; and such a lightly sketched spiritualistic basis might be applied to almost any symphonic work of these movements—*Allegro; Lento; Presto.* The addition of the title "Voluptes," which someone has freely translated "Sensuous Pleasures," to the beautiful *Lento* movement is slightly humorous; it is only sensuous in so far as all musical sound is sensuous in its very essence. Then again if a "Programme" must be admitted, there is no reason or excuse for the full Recapitulations of the Sonata-form; he should have adopted the more pliable Tone-poem form of Liszt and Berlioz. But Scriabin seems to have been obsessed with the strict Sonata-form.

His obsession of the four-bar phrase, too, is quite amazing.

But even viewed entirely as absolute music, the Symphony is too long-drawn. The first movement alone occupies 127 pages of the score. Truly music-making with this Russian is a very serious business. (I feel quite convinced that his projected *Mystery* would have been a three-days' affair.) The Symphony was produced for the first time in Paris on May 29, 1905, under the baton of Arthur Nikisch. The full score was published by Belaieff in the same year, and in 1908 Mr. Léon Conus made a very fine four-handed arrangement of the work for the piano.

The "Poem of Ecstasy," Opus 54, in C

The *Poem of Ecstasy* was begun in Beattenberg during the late summer of 1907, and was finished in January, 1908. As a by-product of the work he immediately wrote off his *Fifth Sonata* in the space of four days, so that these two works may be said to have a psychological relationship. The composition was first performed at the Third Symphonic Concert at Moscow in 1909, under the baton of Safonoff. It gained the Second Prize in the annual competition in honour of Glinka, founded by Belaieff; the First Prize of this year going to Rachmaninoff for his Symphony, a work of much longer proportions. The work had a mixed reception, the chief reviewer of the leading Moscow musical journal heaping personal abuse on the composer; whilst the assistant reviewer shortly after wrote a glowing tribute on Scriabin's musical creations.

The work is scored for a completely modern symphonic orchestra, the Wood-wind laid out in groups of three, with additions of Piccolo, English Horn, Bass Clarinet, and Double Bassoons, the Brass comprising 8 Horns in F, 3 Trumpets in B flat, and the usual Trombones and Tuba. The percussion includes Tuned Drums, Bass Drum, Cymbals, Triangle, Gong, Clochettes (little bells), Cloche (large bell), Celesta; there are also two Harps and Organ. The String section is necessarily a large one, being much sub-divided, and it includes some prominent passages also for a Solo Violin.

The plan on which the work is constructed is one much favoured by the composer. Prologue (containing the two leading motives); Sonata form proper; Epilogue. I give the general outline.

(*a*) Prologue, *Andante, Lento*, Orchestral Score, pages 3 to 8. (Piano Arrangement, pages 3 to 6.)

(*b*) Sonata form proper, *Allegro volando*, Full Score, page 9. (Piano Arrangement, page 7.)

(*c*) Development portion, *Allegro*, Full Score, page 29. (Pianoforte Arrangement, page 17.)

(*d*) Recapitulation, Full Score, page 58, *Allegro volando*. (Piano Arrangement, page 33.)

(*e*) Coda *Allegro molto*, Full Score, page 88. (Pianoforte Arrangement, page 49.)

The basic idea of this the fourth chief orchestral work of Scriabin is the Ecstasy of untrammelled action, the Joy in Creative Activity. The Prologue contains the following two motives, which may be said to symbolise: (*a*) human striving after the ideal;

(*b*) the Ego Theme gradually realising itself.

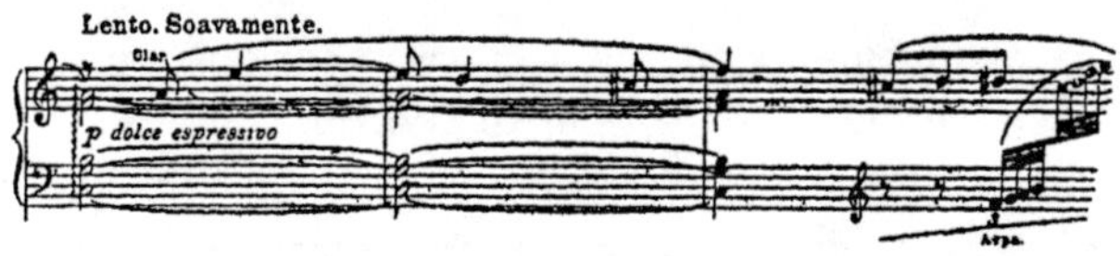

The Sonata-form proper starts with the following subject, symbolic of the soaring flight of the spirit.

The leading motives of the Prologue are almost immediately brought into conjunction with it.

The second subject *Lento* is of a dual character, the higher theme on a violin solo being marked *carezzando*, and apparently typifying Human Love, whilst the lower theme is marked *serioso :*

The third subject then enters an imperious trumpet theme summoning the Will to rise up.

The creative force appears in rising sequences of fourths, having a close affinity to the corresponding theme in *Prometheus.*

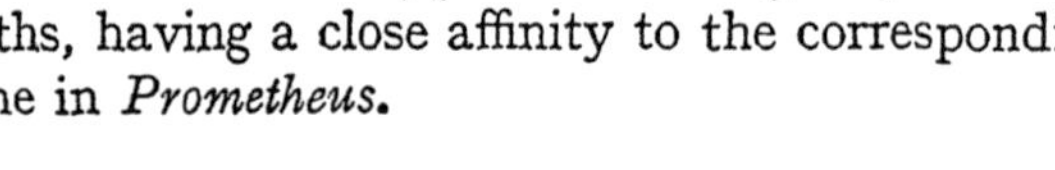

The themes grow in force and pass through moods of almost kaleidoscopic duration—at times spending dreamy moments of delicious charm and perfume, occasionally rising to climaxes of almost delirious pleasure; at other moments experiencing violent stormy emotions and tragic cataclysms. In the development we pass through moments of great stress :

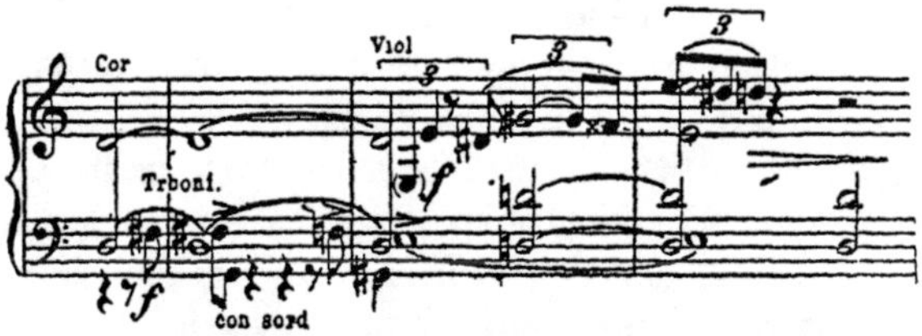

and only achieve brief snatches of the happier mood. Defiant phrases cut right down across the calmer motives, the second of which appears in full as a Prologue to the Recapitulation section. The three subjects are repeated in full, followed by moods of the utmost charm :

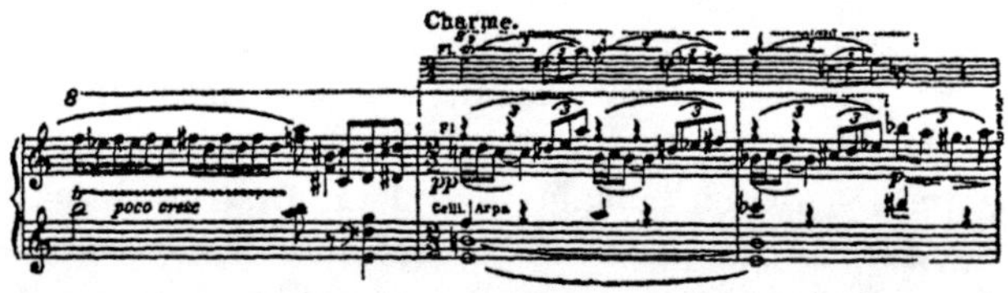

and pleasurable feelings becoming more and more ecstatic, even *Scherzando,* at length reaching an *Allegro molto* Coda of the swiftest and lightest flight imaginable. The Trumpet subject becomes broader, and assumes great majesty, until it finally unrolls itself in a rugged and diatonic Epilogue of immense power and triumphant grandeur.

. . . . . .

The harmonic system of this work may be said

to be on the border-line between the first period of the composer's harmonic technique and his final one. The newer harmony is not continuous, but is here used in conjunction or rather in alternation with the old. The Coda is almost (not quite) old-fashioned in its broad diatonic style, being completely devoid of chromaticism. The composition serves as an excellent illustration of the manner in which Scriabin's more advanced harmony sprang logically and evolved gradually from the older method.

We have attempted a psychological explanation of the music—an almost unavoidable course, seeing that it is outlined in the composer's French indications, and that he pursues the same methods, the very same moods, occasionally even the same melodic subject (*cf.* the Trumpet Theme with that in *Prometheus*), as he does in his other symphonic works. But Scriabin, notwithstanding all his explainers and annotators (blessed word!), is the champion of absolute music—music pure and simple—read what you like into it. As Schumann says, "Intelligence may err; but sensibility cannot."

We have then in this imposing symphonic creation a piece of wonderful beauty, full of rich themes, well developed and combined, with masterly counterpoint and modern harmony of a hue of which the like has not been heard before. It is musically logical, full of contrast, design, and colour. At times the texture is quite simple; at other moments of great complexity. Altogether it is a work of great originality and high poesy—an epoch-making work in the handling of modern harmony; far outstripping Strauss, Stravinsky, and all the rest of the moderns in this respect.

"Prometheus: The Poem of Fire," Opus 60, in F sharp

This Tone-poem (which, by the way, is on Symphony lines) is the last orchestral work which the master has left us. It was commenced when he was residing in Brussels in 1909, but it was not finished until after his final return to Moscow, where he settled in April, 1910. The striking design which appears on all the covers of the music copies of *Prometheus* was drawn by Monsieur Jean Delville, the leader of the theosophist cult in Brussels, to which circle I believe Scriabin belonged; or at any rate he was closely connected with the members of it.

The poetic basis of the music forms one of the most ancient stories of Grecian mythology. The story of Prometheus probably goes back much further than the times of Homer and Hesiod; indeed it seems to come from a period coeval with the dawn of human consciousness itself. Beethoven has treated the legend in his overture *The Men of Prometheus*, but the form of his legend is very much more modern and less primitive than that adopted by Scriabin. With that love of primitive folk-law and with feelings untrammelled by the culture of the west, Scriabin, like his compatriot Stravinsky, goes right to the very mainsprings of the myth. His Prometheus is one of those "Sons of the Flame of Wisdom " who were concerned with the spiritual side of mankind, and who in the remotest ages imparted to man the sacred spark which gradually grew and developed into human intelligence and personality.

According to the explainers of this myth, ethnology proceeded somewhat on these lines: mankind in its incipient stages, unillumined by the Promethean spark, imperfectly formed physically, was originally devoid of self-consciousness. That is "without Karma." On the reception of the Promethean spark they passed to the stage of human consciousness and creative power. But only the more advanced rightly understood the gift and used it on the higher spiritual planes. They became the sages and seers of later ages. Those more ignorant and less advanced in the scale of evolution, on the other hand, turned the gift to gross purposes and so brought suffering and evil into the world. Thus the Promethean gift of the fire of consciousness and intelligence brought both good and evil into the world, proving both a blessing and a curse.

Prometheus is scored for an orchestra of large dimensions, in which the solo pianoforte plays a prominent part; the Wood-wind instruments are all treated in threes—3 Flutes, 3 Oboes, 3 Clarinets, 3 Bassoons, *plus* Piccolo, English Horn, Bass Clarinet, and Double Bassoon. The Brass is a very full band, consisting of 8 Horns in F, 5 Trumpets in B flat, 3 Trombones and Tuba. Besides this there are the usual Strings, which are frequently subdivided into eight and even ten parts. A solo violin is also used. But we have by no means finished; for there is a very elaborate accessory division of percussion instruments. In addition to the usual Tuned Drums, there is the Bass Drum, Cymbals, Gong, Triangle, Campanelli (small bells), written in the one-foot register, but sounding still an octave higher like the piccolo, and requiring two executants, (*campane*) heavy bells. In addition to all we have parts for 2 Harps, and (for the Coda) Organ and Mixed Chorus of voices.

The most original addition to the orchestra is the *Tastiera per Luce*—a keyboard of coloured light-rays invented by the Englishman, Rimington.[1] The performer on this new optical instrument plays on a piano-like keyboard from an ordinary treble stave of an octave in compass. Here is a specimen of his part:

This instrument plays a continuous *rôle* from the beginning to the end of the Symphony, but it is only fair to say that the composer gives a printed authority that where such elaborate means are not available, "*Prometheus* may be performed without 'clavier à lumières' and without Chorus."

It has been stated that the Pianoforte part is supposed to personify the microcosm *Man*, in contrast to the microcosm of the *Cosmos* represented by the orchestra, but I think this idea hinders rather than helps the correlation of the various subjects and their combination. One rather

[1] See page 226

amusing feature at the first London performance, if we except this *rôle* for the piano, was the fact that the unfortunate flatness of the pianoforte pitch unnecessarily emphasised the frailty of the human side of things as contrasted with the more exalted *rôle* of the orchestra.

Remarkable to relate, even with so complex a programme, Scriabin adheres to his life-long admiration of the "classical form" as displayed in the Sonatas and Symphonies of Beethoven. The "planning out" of this work is as follows:

(*a*) Exposition containing nine motives or themes, pages 3 to 23 of the full score. (Pages 3 to 22 of the piano arrangement.)

(*b*) Development beginning with the opening theme on page 23, full score up to page 56. (Pages 22 to 43, piano arrangement.)

(*c*) Recapitulation second theme on page 56, full score. (Page 43, piano arrangement.)

(*d*) Coda prestissimo, full score, page 73. (Piano arrangement, page 56.)

The work opens *Lento* with a characteristic Scriabinic chord (root F sharp).

Lento. Brumeux. M.M ♩= 60

The atmosphere is nebulous and mystical, and the following basic theme is gently breathed forth by the horns, intended to suggest a crepuscular, invertebrate state of Karma-less humanity.

This is succeeded by an imperious trumpet call—the awakening of the will to create. It does not at first appear in its complete form. This is followed by a striking harmonic theme, contemplative in mood and symbolical of dawning consciousness.

Again the summoning trumpet call rings out across the primordial chaos, and the Joy of Life enters with the piano figure.

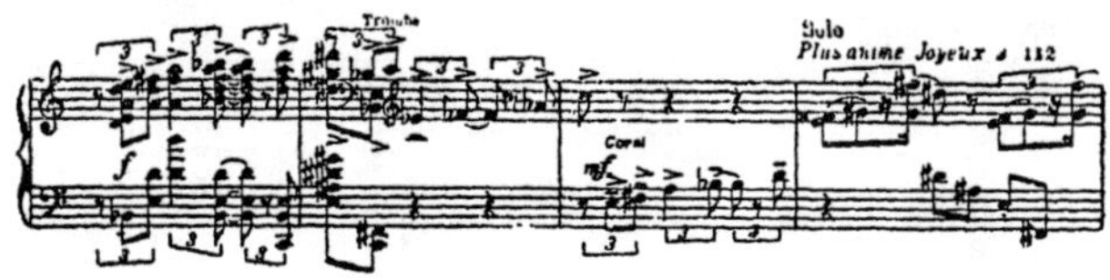

Alas, with the stirrings of self-consciousness come many perplexities, a vague desire for a more intense life, an increase of fresh pristine joy. Languor is also felt.

Human love springs forth in the wake of the Promethean gift.

Joy and pain commingle, and the world-old conflict between the physical and spiritual comes into being. Development continues until we come to the full broad majesty of the opening theme of the whole work, which may be taken as the EGO or "personality" subject proper.

A new theme enters on the violins, marked with enthusiasm; but this is soon confronted by a sinister menacing fragment of the opening theme on muted trumpets. The piano re-enters with an ardent phrase. The development is far too complicated to be followed closely here, but some idea of the moods which it passes may be gained by a glance at the following motives:

Some are of exquisite beauty, others informed by a distorted harmony, or by an almost revolting dissonance. Limpid passages of exquisite beauty succeed imperious trumpet themes; sudden moments of sweet and joyous ravishment of the ear are met with defiant bellicose motives and stormy episodes. Brilliant flashes of orchestration and passages like a cry wrung out by pain pass across this marvellous orchestral canvas which glows with such wild beauty and striking tragedy.

The "Return" section, bathed in a luminous glow, contains many rapturously ecstatic passages

The themes now reach their full development, culminating in a *Prestissimo* of unrestrained palpitating delight.

Human individuality is merged in the Cosmos. Towards the end, after some passages of most striking harmonic beauty and colour, the trumpet theme typifying the " Will to create and attain," enters completely triumphant, and closes in a blaze of harmony on an F sharp major chord.

. . . .

I have shown how the work conforms obediently to the æsthetic rules of logical musical construction. I will now explain briefly how essentially the tonality of the work hangs together on a perfectly logical basis. Let us take the opening chord. Here is its root position. It conforms to the usual formation by fourths, adopted by Scriabin entirely in his third period. We might say that the chord appears at the opening in its fifth inversion with the minor ninth G natural in the bass. The first theme (see page 197) is built entirely out of notes of this chord. Although it seems completely melodic, yet from this view it is a mere arpeggio :—root, 13th, 9th, and so on. The second theme, given also on page 197, is likewise entirely stable in its tonality, F sharp. Whilst the composer holds himself free to take similar harmonies on any of the other eleven diatonic notes,[1] yet you will find that the F sharp harmonic chord retains easily the nature of a tonic centre. The choice of F sharp as the key of the piece will interest those who believe in key colour. I confess I am not one myself, as our variable concert pitch, often to the extent of a semitone, seems to knock the bottom out of this theory entirely.

It is true that the absence of a leading-note in Scriabin's new system often gives the impression of his tonic harmony becoming Dominant in character as in the Pianoforte theme (page 198, No. 2) ; but it is not so really, the impression is only due to our unaccustomed ears. Nearly all the other themes are derived similarly from this Tonic harmony of F sharp.

Prometheus was first produced in Moscow on March 2, 1911, at one of Kussevitzsky's Symphony Concerts. The work met with an enthusiastic

[1] I say " diatonic " as it is of the utmost importance to remember that there is *no such thing* as chromaticism with the modern composers such as Scriabin, Debussy, Ravel, Schönberg, and others.

reception by the supporters, disciples, and followers of Scriabin, but it completely mystified the rest of the audience, who could not understand such a novel kind of music-making. There was indeed an organised section at the concert who hissed and booed and indulged in cat-calls. But this is the fate of a reformer, and during the whole of his lifetime Scriabin suffered annoyance from certain hostile and unsympathetic cliques; on the other hand, he had in Moscow many enthusiastic supporters: Kussevitzsky, Safonoff, Belaieff, Sabanieff, Gunst, and many others. Modernity and progress will always be opposed by routine followers and ignorant conservatism. The work made an immense impression under the baton of Kussevitzsky, with the composer at the piano, although it was not on that occasion done with optical colours. The only occasion on which this was done was in New York in the spring of 1915.

The work was given in London on February 1, 1913, twice at one concert. A number of people mystified or enraged (perhaps both) left the hall after the first hearing; but the majority who stayed for the second part admitted that the work became much clearer at the second hearing. The work was repeated in London in the following year (March 14, 1914) with the composer himself at the piano. The *Musical Times* of April, 1914, wrote:

> "On this occasion the composer himself played the extraordinary pianoforte part, and showed that he possessed fine technique if not great

power. Sir Henry Wood conducted the strange and complex music with much skill, being fortified, no doubt, after his experience derived at the first performances (two at one concert!) last year, and also by the help afforded by personal touch with the composer."

The *Monthly Musical Record* of the same date recorded it thus:

"A crowded audience welcomed M. Alexander Scriabin's first appearance here at the Queen's Hall Symphony Concert of March 14, when that much-discussed composer took the piano parts in two of his own works. The first, the *Piano Concerto* in F sharp minor, numbered Op. 20, is an early work, in which it is not difficult to trace the influences of Chopin and Liszt. Without being particularly distinctive, the Concerto has many eloquent pages, notably in the slow movement, and its regard for form is never carried to the length of formality. In melodic freshness and logical design it presents the strongest contrast to *Prometheus*, which immediately followed it in this programme. It cannot honestly be said that the theosophical complexities of *Prometheus* appeared more intelligible than they did a year ago, when Sir Henry Wood gave us two performances in the same programme. That the work has at times a strange beauty all its own is undeniable, but it is equally true that it contains a good deal that sounds to the uninitiated like mere noise; and, unlike the singing of a certain unmusical Bishop, it is certainly not a 'cheerful noise.' Unmistakable signs of disapproval mingled with the applause at the end, but they were eventually drowned in the appreciated applause of those who apparently recognised the truth of M. Scriabin's picture of the struggle of man from 'the crepuscular, invertebrate state of Karma-less humanity' to his ultimate phase of development. In both works Scriabin played with a deftness in which there was no trace of virtuosity, and, considering the provocative tendency of his talent, he has every reason to be satisfied with his first appearance before an English audience."

If the critics as a whole failed to recognise the real importance of the work, there were, on the other hand, numbers of keen musical appreciators amongst the audience who undoubtedly did have some perception of the really great ideas and thoughts lying beneath this novel yet beautiful web of sound.

XII

THE LATER PIANO PIECES (OPP. 52 TO 74)

"No man putteth new wine into old wine-skins."

I MUST again draw attention to the unsatisfactoriness of drawing any fixed lines of demarcation in the divisions of Scriabin's creations. Whilst divisions of some sort are helpful in getting a right estimate of the whole of his art-work, yet they must be regarded as only roughly approximate, as some of these later pieces might reasonably be placed in the middle period, whilst many of the charming numbers between Opp. 40 and 50 approach very near to the final stage—Op. 48, for instance. Some would perhaps prefer a larger number of even rougher divisions, say, Opp. 1 to 20, student period; 21 to 30, more mature pieces; 31 to 40, masterpieces in the old style; 41 to 50, transition works; 51 to 60, new style; 61 to 74, most advanced works.

Whatever divisions we may choose to adopt, certainly the *Fifth Sonata*, Op. 52, marks an epoch in his work. I have discussed this work in Chapter X. In it we see a new, or shall we say rather a more definite basis for his inspiration and creation. The motto prefaced to the work is a quotation from the *Poem of Ecstasy*, which is probably a poetical production much admired by the Theosophists. This has led annotators astray to the extent of considering Scriabin a writer of the kind of music which is clumsily termed "Programme Music," and which describes a definite series of events in a form of art which undoubtedly leads to the modern realism in music of Strauss and others.

The Sonatas undoubtedly have a close connection with these separate pieces, some long, but most of them short, where we have, however, a much more delightful way of getting to know Scriabin. In these pieces we have one or more of his many moods developed and contrasted with little attempt to relate them to one another. In the Sonatas we find a fixed evolutionary course in which Scriabin explains the Cosmos. There are only two exceptions to this amongst the loose pieces; the *Poème-Nocturne* in D flat (Op. 61), and Op. 70, *Vers la Flamme* (Towards the Flame). In these he follows in the same lines as in the Sonatas, but more pleasantly, I think (see page 209).

These shorter pieces are not theosophic expositions, or great spiritual dramas, but just the expression of one or more moods, mere fancies of great delicacy, charm, or force, as the case may be. Safonoff describes them as "each like a flower out of whose depths a firefly shakes his light." Then there are studies, light sketches, pastels, and fantastic records where it is just as though the composer says: "Pray do not take these delicate mosaics of the air too seriously; I spin them out gossamer-like for my own amusement."

With Taine, writing of the author of *The Merchant of Venice,*[1] we can imagine Scriabin saying, "My brain, being full of fancies, desires to make play of them. Here they are—this is the medley of forms, colours, sentiments, which I shuffle and single before me, a many-tinted skein of glistening silks, a slender arabesque, whose sinuous curves, crossing and confused, bewilder the mind by the whimsical variety of their infinite complications."

Like R. L. Stevenson in his languorous moments, it was probably not the end which pleased Scriabin so much as the journey itself.

. . . . . .

Let us first take the *Poème-Nocturne,* Op. 61. It is without key-signature, but it is in the tonality of D flat. In the final chord which lingers delicately on the ear, both the minor 9th and the major 9th appear together. It opens with a capricious grace:

Then come episodes, *comme une ombre mouvante, comme un murmure confus, avec une volupté dormante,*

[1] It is interesting to note that some critics attribute Shakespeare's *Merchant of Venice* to a Buddhist origin.

comme en un rêve, and so on. Then the chief subject appears :

a moment of languor follows, only to be followed by the irresistible blossoming out of the chief theme, mounting higher and higher; then it all comes over again, the capricious grace, the moving shade, the confused murmur, the sleeping senses, and the clear theme of personality—an exact repeat, because this composer is such a lover of form and design. Poor evolution, truly—but exquisite music.

The logic is much sounder in Op. 72, *Vers la Flamme*,[1] which is in every way quite one of his best works. This commences with sombre shades :

The music gradually acquires more and more life, light, and rhythm until the chief subject is clearly defined; this grows more and more luminous and brilliant, finally ending in a climax of blazing

[1] Said to have been intended to form part of a Sonata.

radiance which requires three staves for its full display.

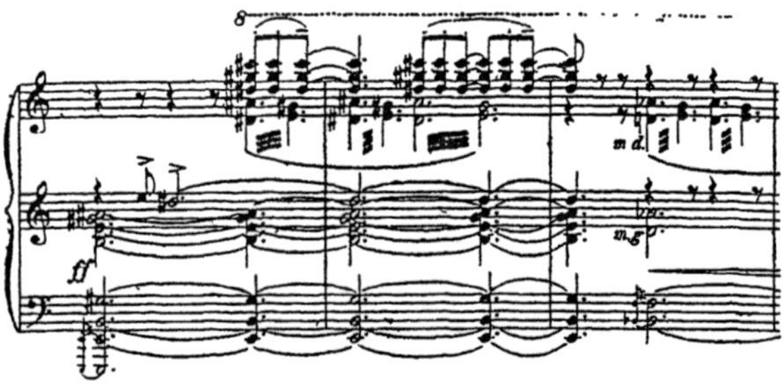

This is rather exacting on the player; and the last chord is a real study for the theorists. The piece is of course in E, but in these higher excursions into harmonics, the customary key signature has long been transferred to limbo.

Op. 52 is an interesting set closely related to the *Poem of Ecstasy*.[1] The first piece contains much beautiful harmony. The time signatures are somewhat confused.[2] Take the piece to a crotchet beat throughout. The cadence is exquisite.

The key-signature of the *Enigma* (No. 2) certainly makes it appear to end on the Dominant, and this marks it distinctly as a piece belonging to

[1] Like it, they were originally published privately by Scriabin, in 1908.

[2] See, however, V. Karatigin's metrical analysis of it.

the transitional stage. The two figures used are those associated by Scriabin with " Soaring Flight " and with the " Dawn of Consciousness."

The carrying of the key-signature is a decided strain on No. 3, *Poème Languide.* The close is of such beauty that it should convince sceptics of the soundness of the composer's use of the higher harmonics. But let tyros beware!

Another attractive set is Op. 56. The first piece, *Violent*, well marked, is full of augmented 6ths on the minor 2nd of the key—a chord much favoured by another Russian, Tchaikovsky (and a younger Belgian, Joseph Jongen), but never taken in such inversions before. It is a magnificent rage: the rage of an Othello or a King Lear; I find schoolboys love this new harmony. No. 2, *Ironies,* a lively *Scherzoso,* is one of the most fantastic things Scriabin has written. Caricatured harmony alternates with caressing sweetnesses. Wonderful to relate, it ends on a plain common chord. Here is one of its lovely episodes:

Nuances is a soft velvety Prelude, the inner parts moving mostly in major 3rds. The *Étude*, No. 4, is the first piece in which he abandons the customary key-signature. But do not imagine for one moment that Scriabin lets go of his key or tonality. The possibilities of the new duodecuple system are inexhaustible.

Twenty years ago I remember reading in the *Musical Times*, London, a long correspondence with the title " Is music played out ? " Certainly not ; but the kind which they meant is. Bach, Beethoven, and Brahms did that for them.

The *Feuillet d'Album,* which appears in the *New Russian Album,* is chiefly interesting from the fact that it is one of the very few pieces which show Scriabin's style of pedalling, which was such a wonderful feature of his playing. Its position in this Album allows an instructive comparison with the pianoforte writing of his old master, Taneieff.

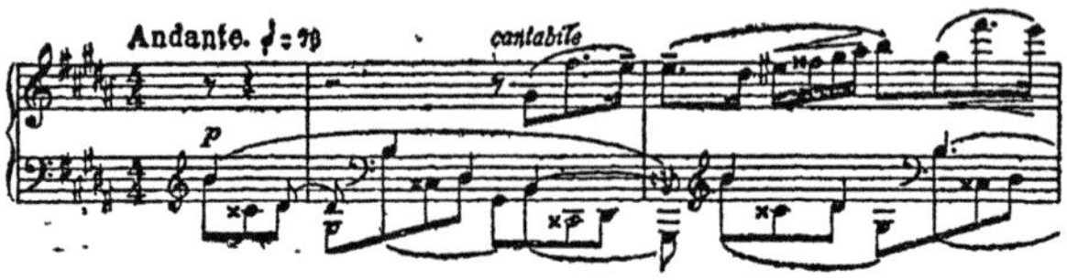

The two pieces of Op. 57 represent the " Longing " mood and the dance element, here carried a stage further into the harmonic region.

The *Masque* and *L'Étrangeté* (Strangeness), Op.

63, are two numbers much favoured by the English pianist, Mr. Leonard Borwick. Now the key-signature is dropped, Scriabin can forge ahead. There are three very interesting examples of French "double-lining" in Op. 65, one in 5ths; one in major 7ths; and, yes, one in 9ths! A very good example of how visualising Scriabin's music may be is afforded by No. 2 of Op. 67. I often play this on the organ with one hand on a soft *Vox Humana* mixture, and the other on a fluttering flute stop or *Unda Maris*. Some hearers visualise fluttering colours during this piece; others see sombre flames; whilst one hearer saw hundreds of multi-coloured night moths fluttering about in the semi-darkness.

Another delightful fantasy of three passing moods alternating kaleidoscopically, begins with four bars of airy capricious flight, then a tenderly drawn melody of four bars, a little fluttering trill, and a fantastic diminution of it. These transient moods change in a most delightful way, like mirages dancing over rippling water.

The mysterious bell-tones of the *Eighth Sonata* have crept into the *Poem*, Op. 71.

Two dance numbers, *Guirlandes* and *Flammes sombres*, Op. 73, have also a very strong visualising power.

The Op. 75, *Five Preludes*, is the last offering which Scriabin has left us. They were written just before his death, and it is possible they give us the sort of language he intended to use for his Mystery. There is always something very touching about the swan-songs of composers, their very last musical breath, whether we take the "Wenn wir in höchsten Nöthen sein" Choral-prelude of Bach, or the set of *Solemn Preludes* for the Organ by Brahms, the *Requiem* of Mozart, or this final set of Scriabin, all finished in the very chamber of departure. Music apparently becomes then more than ever a part of a man's soul; and here the words of Carlyle come in with peculiar force.

> "Music is well said to be the speech of angels; in fact nothing among the utterances allowed to mankind is felt to be so divine. It brings us near to the Infinite, we look for moments, across the cloudy elements, into the Eternal Sea of Light."

The first four of these final Preludes are very gloomy in their perverse—one might almost say deliberately distorted—harmonic expression, but the fifth redeems them. . . . We do well to remember here that for the last year of his life Scriabin was haunted by premonitions of some indefinable fate hanging over him. The first is marked "Sad, heart-rending," and certainly it is so. Here is the final phrase.

The piece is only 16 bars; such poignancy cannot go on for long. The second Prelude of this farewell set is full of a great soughing as of the wind over bleak moors. It strains our modern chromatic scale almost to breaking point, requiring an enharmonic instrument with a scale like Busoni's tertia-tonal one (18 sounds to the octave) rather than our 12-note tuning. Still, on account of its pervading Tonic-sound in the bass, it is more acceptable than the other later pieces. The third Prelude is more violent in its proud indignant outcry against trouble and grief. Although marked *Allegro dramatico* it is only 26 bars long. The fourth contains 24 bars of the most cacophonous harmony ever written by this most illusive of composers. It is marked *lent, vague, indecis.* Has he passed beyond the possibilities of our musical system, or did his fine mental grip of things loosen its moorings just for one brief moment? I cannot say. The very last piece is proud and bellicose. The harmony is exceedingly advanced and sounds even more complex than it is, on account of the delayed appearance of the Tonic Chord (bar 4). It ends with a half-cadence—the diminished fifth being reckoned as the Dominant.

Now the Half-cadence at the end of a piece is regarded as a Question—a significant Question too, this! . . .

XIII

MUSIC AND COLOUR

> *"Non, la musique n'est pas un instrument de plaisir physique. La musique est un des produits les plus delicats de l'esprit humain. Dans les profondeurs de son intelligence, l'homme possède un sens intime spécial, le sens esthétique, par lequel il perçoit l'art; la musique est un des moyens de mettre ce sens en vibration."*
>
> *Camille Saint-Saens.*

AMONGST the strangest manifestations in the mental energies of the last half-century are the many attempts to combine Art and Science; and even two apparently unrelated arts themselves. The problem of the Opera—a would-be perfect combination of drama and music—is still unsolved despite the efforts of the last three hundred years—Gluck, Wagner, and Debussy notwithstanding. A new art—the *mimique*, or wordless play, with music of Wormser and Rébikoff—and the "ballet" (as understood by the Russians) promises to be a serious rival to the form now known as Opera.

We have already discussed Scriabin's relation of Musical Harmony to the principles of Acoustics. Such an attempt is not surprising. Painters have developed on similar lines.[1]

Scriabin's own master, Taneieff, wrote an ex-

[1] Georges Seurat, Paul Signac, and others.

ceedingly clever treatise correlating Mathematics (algebra) and Musical Counterpoint, and always taught Musical Composition on those lines at the Moscow Conservatoire. We have already mentioned (page 51 *et seq.*) several artists who had similar aims. But although in Brussels many philosophers had vaguely referred to a possible relationship, no composer until Scriabin had ever thought of making (or should we say dared to make ?) the experiment.

A brief record of the former glances in this direction may be interesting.

First the Scientists. Dr. Maclean, in the *I.M.S. Zeitschrift*, April, 1913, gives a summary of the inventions which led men to think of a closer approximation of Light and Sound. In the *Telephone* (1861, Philipp Reis of Friedrichshof; 1876, Alexander Graham Bell, of Edinburgh, Würzburg, and Boston), sound acting on a vibrating metal diaphragm at one end of a wire is reproduced as sound on a vibrating metal diaphragm at the other end of the wire, the transmitting agency over the wire being the rapid intermittances of electromagnetism. The action is augmented by use of the *Microphone* (1878, David Edward Hughes, of Barktown College, Kentucky), where carbon-surfaces in juxtaposition intensify the electrical resistances at the transmitting end. All this is now commonplace, and an incident of practical life.

In the *Photophone* (1880, Graham Bell), sound acting on the back of a very thin diaphragm-like plane glass mirror travels to a distance (not over a

see how the two things can be compared physically, since: (*a*) light travels through ether, sound will not; (*b*) the speed of transference of sound-vibration is infinitesimal compared with that of light.

Now for the Philosophers. The recognition of some analogy between Colour and Sound dates back from the time of Aristotle; but nothing of value was attained. Even Rameau and Grétry in the seventeenth and eighteenth centuries confine themselves to generalising. Referring to a "colour-harpsichord," invented by Father Castel, a Jesuit, Grétry says: "A sensitive musician will find all colours in the harmony of sound. The solemn or minor keys will affect his ear in the same way that gloomy colours affect his eye; and the sharp keys will seem like bright and glaring colours. Between these two extremes one may find all the other colours which are contained in music just as they are in painting, and belong to the expression of different emotions and different characters."

Mr. Edison, the monarch of mechanical sound, has achieved what will probably be his last and greatest triumph, by means of the *Kinetophone*. This is a talking-machine that works in conjunction with moving pictures. The idea is to get theatrical companies to give performances, which can then be carried and sent to all parts of the world. When put in operation, not only is the spectacle to be seen on the canvas, but the actors' voices will be reproduced faithfully and at the precise chronological moment. Of course, the two contrivances have been worked separately for a long time, but it has taken Mr. Edison four years to bring about their combination in such a way that an exact representation, optical and aural, can be given. At first sight, this may not appear difficult nowadays, but when one remembers that the words have to be heard fitting exactly, so to speak, the movements of the actors' mouths on the sheet, forming thus practically a perfect reduplication of the original performance, Mr. Edison's accomplishment will be appreciated. Whether it is likely to affect the actor's or operatic artist's calling is another matter, though there is no need for, say, Sir Herbert Tree to travel to Manitoba to give his impersonation of Falstaff, when the inhabitants can see and hear him by potted mechanism. We do not think it will injure the finances of the theatrical profession, for, after all, people prefer to see their popular performers in the flesh. Rather will it be a great boon to those comparatively obscure centres where there is no possibility of famous performers paying a visit. It is all very wonderful.

An American scientist, Dr. Lee de Forest, claims that he can produce musical sounds from light by means of an instrument which he has invented. The *Audion Amplifier*, which has made wireless telephony an accomplished fact, is utilised for this purpose, and just as the faint vibrations are caught by the wireless detector, and amplified to a powerful degree, so, it is claimed, can the light-giving particles that vibrate at the rate of a hundred million times per second be transmitted into sound.

The Audion is an instrument resembling an ordinary electric light bulb, but having certain internal modifications.

Years ago Dr. de Forest discovered that when the circuits of the Audion were connected in a certain way a clear musical note was heard in a telephone receiver connected in one of these circuits. The quality, he said, was beautiful, having a highly developed fundamental, with few upper partials, but he found, after a little experimenting, that he was able to change the upper partials, and thus to vary the quality. The pitch of the notes could likewise be altered by changing the induction in the circuits. The next step was the arranging of a crude scale similar in function to that of an organ with switches in place of keys. An instrument with a hundred bulbs would be no larger than a "talking machine cabinet," and the console would be about the size of a typewriter. The inventor now hopes to produce an instrument so far perfected that he can turn it over to musicians to work out the thousand and one details of musical perfection which such men alone are capable of introducing.

A red herring is drawn across the trail by people who attach colours to the various keys or scales. Rameau was vague. In his *Traité de l'Harmonie reduite à ses Principes naturels*, 1722, he writes: "The major mode, taken in the octave of the notes C, D, or A, is suited to lively and joyful airs; in the octave of the notes F or B flat, it is suited to tempests and anger, and subjects of that kind. In the octave of the notes G or E, it is suited to songs of a gentle or gay nature; also in the octave of D, A, or E, what is great and magnificent may find expression. The minor mode, taken in the octave of D, G, B, or E, is suited to tenderness and love; in the octave of C or F, to tenderness and sadness."

Grétry got a step further when he remarked that the scale of emotions was common to that of colour and sound, for the expression of different emotions brought different colours to the face. "Purple red indicates anger; a paler red accompanies shyness," etc.

No sort of agreement has yet been reached as to the manner of applying the scale of colours to the musical scale. One experimenter will apply a colour scale to the eight diatonic musical notes, and suggests variations of the hues for the chromatic alteration. Another will use different hues for the twelve notes of the octave, with different shades of the same hues for the octave above. This aspect of the subject was developed by Dr. D. D. Jameson in his *Colour Music* (Smith and Elder, 1844); in 1869, by J. D. Macdonald, *Sound and Colour* (Longmans); by F. J. Hughes in *Harmonics of Tones and Colours* (1883); by G. B. Allen, *Scales in Music and Colours*; and by Mr. G. W. Rimington in *The Art of Mobile Colour* (Hutchinson, 1911).

The latter was prepared to put his Scale to the severest tests; and on June 6, 1895, he invited people to witness his symphonies of colour played from musical scores on his own "colour keyboard."

The so-called "colour organ"[1] may be briefly described as a large box fitted with a number of apertures, which are filled in with varied hued glass. These apertures are illumined from within the box, and are opened and shut by mechanism acted upon by a pianoforte keyboard, but which emits no sound. Each note in the octave is allotted a certain tint chosen from the spectrum band (commonly recognised in the rainbow), the colours of each note being decided by the analogy which exists between the number of vibrations by which the ear recognises the pitch, and the number of vibrations which the eye has to receive before it can distinguish any particular tint. Thus the note middle C on the keyboard is associated with what is scientifically known as the "low" red; the next hue is given to C sharp, and so on through the rainbow shades until the deep violet is reached with the seventh note of the scale; low red being repeated for the octave C, and the series of colours recommenced. This is ingenious, although scarcely new, but its further application to sound is arbitrary, and in several respects the system is a distinct failure. The fact that representations of pitch are confined to the octave at once shows the inadequacy of the plan.

The working method pursued was for a piece to be played on a pianoforte next to the colour-organ, and for an assistant to play simultaneously the same piece on its dumb keyboard. When this was done the colours associated with the notes were thrown upon a white sheet. When chords were

[1] *Musical News*, June 15, 1895.

struck several tints were thrown on the sheet at once, the result being that many of the richest harmonies produced a muddy white, instead of the rich hues which psychologically were expected. Many of the colour changes were, moreover, crude in the extreme, and when the notes were played at all rapidly, the effect was almost blinding. Mr. Rimington had provided an orchestra, which, however, still more glaringly manifested the inadequacy of the "new art"(?) to represent sound by colour. A trumpet note conveys a different idea from the same note sounded *pianissimo* by the strings, but the colour-organ blazons forth both with equal intensity. In other words, it is utterly incapable of conveying the effects of timbre. In his endeavours to associate colour and sound, Mr. Rimington has overlooked the fact that the capability of the eye to recognise rapid changes is far less than that possessed by the ear; that whereas the retina of the eye retains the image thrown upon it for the sixth part of a second, to the exclusion of a fresh image, the ordinary ear will recognise changes of pitch and timbre with a rapidity almost beyond capability of calculation. The title "colour music" can, therefore, scarcely with justice be applied to Mr. Rimington's ingenious arrangement of colour representations. Mobility of colour, to be grateful, must obviously from the construction of our organs of sight be restricted to comparatively slow changes, and thus colour under the most elaborate manipulation can only be associated with a very limited portion of musical effects, and that but distantly. In short, all Mr. Rimington's machine did was to produce, now and again, apart from any musical significance, some pretty shades of fine tints, but nothing approaching in beauty to those seen at recent exhibitions at which coloured lights were thrown upon fountains. Rimington maintains that colour discords can be phrased and resolved just as musical discords and also analysed, for any skilled painter can of course resolve a compound colour with certainty into its components. But in actual practice the degree of dissonance between the colour discords and the musical discords was widely divergent.

Scriabin adopted Rimington's colour-keyboard for his *Prometheus*, a dual Symphony of Sound and Colour—two Symphonies at once in fact. He, however, used a Colour Scale of his own, founded on the piano-tuner's "cycle of fifths," and wrote music in a novel harmonic and scientific system to give the colour-symphony a fair opportunity of making its effect.

These twelve hues he placed on a small twelve-note keyboard on the lines of Rimington's, and depended on one, two, or three various hues combined for his "colour-symphony." These colour harmonies followed more or less closely the bass notes of his novel harmonies, and the same colours are preserved for the same harmonies. Since colour changes must not be quick if they are to be distinctly seen and not become merely blinding, Scriabin's new system of composing was eminently fitted for the dual symphonising. At the Moscow and London performances *Prometheus* was given without Colour, but at the New York presentation the work was given with every detail carefully carried out.

Mr. Clarence Lucas, writing in the *Musical Courier* in characteristic American style, says: "During the performance of the orchestral score the lights in the auditorium were extinguished, and a white sheet at the back of the platform and above the heads of the players was illuminated by streaks and spots of light of various colours which had no possible connection with the music, but which served to divert the senses of the audience from a too concentrated attention on the music. Scriabin, therefore, succeeded in making his music heard in exactly the same way that operatic music in general is heard—that is to say, by a divided attention. This *Prometheus* music of Scriabin is not at all extraordinary or absurd when heard under the conditions intended by the composer. Nearly every chord was recognisable by a trained ear—chords of the ninth, with altered fifths, secondary and diminished sevenths, with passing notes and suspensions, and so on. But there was plenty of free, though intelligible counterpoint, and much variety of orchestral combinations of sounds."

The difficulty in applying colour to music is increased by the confusion of ideas in its manner of relationship. Some connect the various colours with the various single notes; others will give certain colours to certain keys or scales. Scriabin's evident preference for the key of F sharp major seems to point to some connection of this sort in his mind. With the first method people may well ask what happens to a piece when the piece is transposed, say, a whole tone up. With the second method comes the reply, pieces should not be transposed at all, but should always appear in the original key as first imagined by the composer. Many composers have not this absolute perception of key.

The right connection, however, between colour and music must be rather on psychic lines. A certain harmony, not a single note, produces a certain effect on the mind; the corresponding colour, which produces a similar effect, is evidently related to it. The common mistake, however, is to imagine that the known physical laws and rules will produce the result. This is not the case of practical experience, however.

Miss Finetta Bruce, in her *Mysticism and Colour* (W. Rider and Co.), describes the Scale of Colour thus:

Grey	Depression
Drab	Gloom
Ashy White	Fear
Reddish Black	Hatred
Black	Despair
Ugly Green	Jealousy
Brown	Selfishness
Dirty Crimson	Anger
Peacock Blue	Vanity and Pride
Blackish Green	Treachery
Rose Red	Love

And the following Octave for Daily Practice :

Red	Life
Orange . . .	Health
Yellow . . .	Wisdom
Green . . .	Energy, Supply, Peace
Blue	Truth
Purple . . .	Power
Amethyst (Mauve) .	Purity
Rose . . .	Love (the 8ve, the same note as Life).

Can the moods of musical composition be tabulated similarly ?

We have not yet, however, stated the whole position. There are already two elements in music which serve the purpose of colour. I refer to orchestral *timbre* or tone-colour, and to chromatic harmony. If, as according to some of our modernists, "middle C" on the piano gives a rich red in their minds, what is to happen when this note is played by a violin or a trumpet ? Then again composers such as Dvorak, Grieg, Chopin, and Liszt are remarkable for their strong and beautiful chromatic colouring. This is the *chroma* of the Greeks, the coloured note of the Middle Ages ; and so the circle comes full.

Music does not gain greatly by such a decided move in the physical direction ; and sooner or later she will find herself in the position of the love-lorn Indian princess, with which allegory I will close this chapter.

A beautiful young Indian princess married a prince after her own heart, but as the years went on and her beauty faded, she thought the affections of her lord were waning, so she prayed the gods to give her surpassing beauty to win back the heart of her prince. This was granted, and the prince's ardour returned. But yet she was not happy, and finally asked that the gift of beauty might be taken away again so that her lord might love her for herself alone.

XIV

FORM AND STYLE

As a rule we do not think of the Russian composers as being exceptionally gifted on the constructional or formal side of music, especially of pure instrumental music. Mussorgsky, Cui, Borodin, and Rimsky-Korsakoff were too much occupied with developing on their own lines when they were not following those three great Romanticists in music—Schumann, Liszt, and Berlioz. Such a course suited their ardent nature, their many moods, much better than the following of traditional designs in composition. Their rejection of the Sonata form too had something of consciousness in it, since it was the outcome of a national stand against the musical dominance of the Germans, who, however, learnt all their form, line, and tonal balance from the beauty-loving Italians.

How then comes it that we find such a reverence for form and design, such a masterly handling of it in Scriabin's music, which is such a wonderful record of an exquisite sensibility, moods changing rapidly from one extreme to the other, from a violent bellicosity to the most winning amiability, from outrageous dissonance to an exquisite sensibility for beautiful tone, from a dreamy meditative introspection to one of aggressive energy. It seems almost unnatural to expect such a nature to pay homage to the demands for the beautiful in design and for the tradition in musical form. Yet he does.

Three things will account for this: the Moscow training, his admiration for Chopin, and his later attachment to the Brussels Theosophist group. The traditions at the Moscow Conservatoire have always been on the side of the eclectics. Men like Tchaikovsky, Arensky, Taneieff, Rachmaninoff, and Ippolitoff Ivan were not the men to let the Conservatoire cripple itself by a too red-hot Chauvinism. The attitude there has always been to draw the best wherever it was to be found. Melody and love of beauty the Moscovites learned from the early Italians, and from the fair land of Italy itself; homophony, counterpoint, and architectural form from Beethoven, Mozart, and Bach; orchestration and harmony from Liszt and Berlioz; and the piano-spirit from Field and Chopin. Later on French influence was to make itself felt there. In Scriabin's larger forms, in the Sonatas and Symphonies, there is something akin to Franck's development of Sonata form. But Scriabin's smaller forms, his Nocturnes, his Preludes, and Studies, were derived directly from the Nocturnes of Chopin, who owed them to the originator, John Field the Englishman. With Chopin, as with Field, the name *Nocturne* became attached to pieces of a similar poetic vein and languorous fancy which were not strictly Evening pieces. The time of gloaming between the sunset and nightfall peculiarly suits such a mood, but the form which fits this mood so perfectly will also express the delicious soliloquies which are born of the lulling, soothing feeling of a rocking boat in a calmly rippling lake, or the delicious dreams in a slowly swinging hammock. The same poetic form served Scriabin admirably for a mountain-top meditation in that wonderful interval which precedes the Dawn when light itself is being born all over again. The intimacy allowed by such a form is its chief merit. "It will never grow old," wrote Liszt of Field's form, "as it is so perfectly adapted to those fleeting impressions which do not belong to that commoner order of sentiments which is bred by one's social environment, but rather to those pure emotional emanations which eternally weave their spell over the heart of man, because he finds them eternally the same whether he is in the presence of the beauties of Nature, or of those soft sweet tendernesses which surround the morning of life, before reflection arrives to darken with her shadow those radiant prisms of feeling. . . . He was a composer who played for himself—and composed for himself." We feel too all this with Chopin, and equally so with Scriabin in his Preludes, Nocturnes, or Poems—call this intimate mould what you will.

Born it was in those hours of the day when the soul, freed from its daily cares, turns solely upon itself and suddenly darts mysteriously into the regions of the starry heavens, with the mind filled with the pure instincts of Childhood itself. Never truly night-pieces, even with Field and Chopin, with Scriabin they are made to fit every hour of the day—matutinal meditations on the mountain tops, sunlight reveries, in blaze of noon, and languorous afternoons. Fancy free as the form is, it is never formless, for perfection and delicacy of finish are inseparable from the form. Sometimes it takes the shape of a single idea dwelt upon fondly and garlanded with arabesques of an Æolian vagueness; at other times it is composed of two ideas, delicately poised and gently oscillating in a sort of Rondo form.

The Miniature form of Chopin's C minor *Prelude* attracted Scriabin, and he wrote many such little pieces, 6 or 16 bars long. The same simplicity of utterance and form characterises his short pieces of the later period, where a short binary or even a unary form serves the requirements of his "mystic chord." But an equal mastery of form is shown in the longer pieces, in his Sonatas and Symphonies. In his earlier Sonatas he shows a strong striving to unify the movements, and in his Third the number has shrunk to two only. His cyclic forms, whether in Symphony or Sonata, show an evolution towards a one-movement form which includes all the properties of the cyclic forms. The exposition of the *Allegro*—the impressiveness of the *Adagio*, the rhythmic appeal of the *Scherzo*, and the animation of the *Finale* are found all gathered up into one complex but unified form.

He was constantly extending the Sonata form to

suit the needs of the moment. His First Sonata commences with a movement of development, followed by a Song-form, a *Presto*, and then a Funeral March. His second has two movements only, a serious Andante and a rushing dancing Presto. The Third Sonata goes back to the form of four movements, a *Dramatico* on development form, an *Allegretto*, an *Andante*, and a final *Presto* un fuoco. There are only two movements—an Andante and a Prestissimo, and both these are connected up into one.

The *Fifth Sonata*, one of his most poetic, is in one-sonata movement with a Prologue and an Epilogue. The last five Sonatas are all in one movement. They are founded on various "mystic" chords and follow theosophic ideas. Thus the second subject typifies the awakening intelligence, and the third, the Ego or Personality theme, becomes the most prominent in the Sonata. Sonata lines of development and recapitulation are still closely followed, the latter, I think, being quite uncalled-for with such a subject. Herein I think Scriabin carried the reverence for the Line and Design of the Belgian school of Modernism too far. Clearness, intelligibility, and beauty can be secured without a recapitulation at variance with the evolution of the subject. Truly, he covers himself with glory at the Coda which, in the later works, either displays the third (chief) subject still more glorified or ends in a dazzling, whirling dance.

Of course every piece need not be "a movement

of development" ; neither need every piece have a climax. Some merely call up a particular emotion or are in fact "picture pieces." They do not need to develop at all, but merely to continue in focus. Many of Scriabin's shorter sketches appear to me as "sky pictures."

One will conjure up a picture of a snow-bound scene just before a December dusk with a pale blue background of sky, banked all round by black-grey clouds, and serenely set in the midst in her queenly beauty is the merest chink of a bright silvery crescent. A single golden star plays the attendant Charmian to her.

Another will be a glorious scintillating summer's afternoon, across which, without warning, tears a terrible thunderstorm. Serried ranks of threatening clouds file rapidly across, rank upon rank. The awesome climax passes and the sunshine reappears, now beautified by the mystic colours of the semi-lucent departing mists.

Like so many others—Coleridge-Taylor, for instance, and York-Bowen—he seems often to have accepted the Beethoven-Mozart Sonata form too blindly. These masters themselves were constantly trying to mould it and never used the full form for slow movements. The blind acceptance of the exactly repeated development, for instance, is a mere fetish. A form of development such as the so-called "Sonata form" is claimed to be—though it never was a stable, but always a mobile form—is illogical. Development of a theme must lead forward—to a higher power—not backward—to a tame and wearisome repetition. What should we think of a rhetorician who, after his development, gave instead of his climax an exact *verbatim* re-statement in full of the first half of his discourse? Re-statement or summary let us have, but not exact or full repetition. It is this needless padding out which is the drawback of Scriabin's first two Symphonies, fine as they are, and it has been damaging in the extreme to such composers as Coleridge-Taylor. Take one of his finest Marches, for instance, "Ethiopia saluting the Colours," into which he put some of his best music. Why did he adopt full Sonata form? And the addition of a third important subject into the Exposition makes the matter even more wearing.

Scriabin's Codas are nearly all of the *Prestissimo* order. The exceptions are when he repeats his slow Prologue as an Epilogue in his Ninth and Tenth Sonatas. The rapid change of strange harmonic bases then makes these climaxes appear some dazzling, aerial, and elusive music as of a dance of air molecules in the intoxication of the sunlight. Gunst would say, "The spirit (or Ego) becomes immersed in the Cosmos." I suppose Mahler has, however, done this sort of thing in his Symphonies, and Debussy has achieved it at least once (in his Fêtes) without any help from a new Theosophy. But the *fons et origo* of all Prestissimo codas is seen in Beethoven's Sonatas Opp. 53 and 54; and they descend directly in evolution from the gigue, which always ended the early Dance Suite. We find the same idea of carrying the listener out of himself at the end of a piece by the sheer impetuosity and speed in many of the organ works of Bach: for instance, the C major Fantasia and Fugue in three movements with its dazzling cadenza-like ending.

Thus we find Scriabin's works in the direct line of development from Bach, Beethoven, Brahms and Liszt.

XV

HIS ORCHESTRATION AND VOCAL WRITING

If one were asked to say in a single word in what department of music the Russians as a race of composers as a whole were pre-eminent, one would at once say orchestration. One thinks of the grandeur and the Velasquian simplicity of colouring in Mussorgsky's operas; the deep feeling for striking tones shown by Rimsky-Korsakoff, the masterly handling of full rich colour (and especially the mezzotints) by Tchaikovsky, the blazing pages of a Stravinsky or a Tscherepnine, and is convinced at once of the remarkable aptitude of the Russian for blending and mixing of tone-colours and of his unerring instinct for the right instrument. Perhaps it is this last intuition which saves them from the extravagances in orchestral requirements of other modern schools, for they are as a rule wonderfully economical in the composition of their orchestras. They are by nature orchestral in feeling, and their string-writing alone always conveys that remarkable feeling of their having put themselves right into the middle of their medium. There is also another reason which may account for their remarkable development of the art of orchestration. The Russian School is one of the youngest of all the schools, and rose at the time when orchestration and the feeling for tone-colour had just entered music.

The Petrograd Conservatoire has always made a special cultivation of instrumentation, and Rimsky-Korsakoff's remarkable book on the principles of orchestration reveals at once one of the most remarkable factors in its development of this subject. Much of his special knowledge was gained by him whilst acting as Government Inspector of Naval Bands, a post he held from 1873 to 1884. Nor must it be forgotten that Rimsky carried on his musical instruction by correspondence with Belaieff throughout his three years' cruise in foreign waters as a naval cadet. He may well have learned his fondness for the cymbals, the triangle, and other percussion instruments from the Celestial Empire itself. Indeed the influence of the East is never entirely absent from the Russian orchestration, but his fondness for bell tones is entirely a National characteristic. Unfortunately his book on orchestration—one of the best since Berlioz—remained unfinished, but dismembered as it is, it is still a most valuable work.

If the study of orchestration was carried on so energetically at the Petrograd Conservatoire it was cultivated no less enthusiastically at Moscow, where the young Scriabin would be formed early on the excellent lines laid down by Tchaikovsky, Nicolas Rubenstein, Taneieff, and G. A. Conus, himself the writer of some fine student textbooks on the subject.

All these considerations would explain the masterly orchestration of Scriabin's early Symphonies and the Piano Concerto. Orchestration seems to have come quite naturally to the young composer as swimming does to the young duckling, but there was probably another great influence on Scriabin in this direction—that of the splendid Belgian Schools whose orchestrators are second only to the Russians. The orchestral traditions at Brussels, Antwerp, Liège, etc., are of a quality unsurpassed even in Paris and London. There were keen professors who were not only developing orchestration on æsthetic and dramatic lines, but were actually endeavouring to incorporate principles of science into the art. I need only mention here the names of such brilliant workers as Gilson, Tinel, Delius, Chatterij, and others. Then again the repertoire at the Brussels Opera and concerts was the most cosmopolitan, open-handed, and eclectic possible. There the operas of all the Russians (Rimsky-Korsakoff, Glazounoff, Tchaikovsky, Taneieff), of the French Masters (Ravel, Magnard, d'Indy, Debussy, Saint-Saëns), and the German (Strauss, etc.), were to be heard; and in the symphonic line the works of Bruckner, Dvorak, Smetana, Mahler, and even Tovey and Elgar.

There are three chief factors which go to the production of good orchestration:

1. The composition and grouping of the instruments.

2. The harmonic disposition of the music played.
3. The acoustic properties of the hall.

In Russia, Scriabin would have learned thoroughly the handling of balance, equilibrium, sonority, and disposition of the orchestral tone mass. He would imbibe there the natural way of writing for instruments, and in Belgium he would hear music in some of the finest acoustic halls in the world.

It is characteristic of Scriabin that the pianoforte plays an important *rôle* in both his first and last orchestral works; but whereas in the favourite early work the orchestral accompaniment forms but a background for the solo instrument, in his final orchestral work, *Prometheus*, the piano becomes merely an integral part of an organic whole.

The first eight bars of the early *Concerto* at once proclaim the composer's fine feeling for orchestral colour and his deft handling of the instruments. Throughout this *Concerto*, the instrumentation is simple yet masterly. Only in the third (final) movement, do we find a little weakness in the treatment of the orchestral basses. There are many picturesque touches, notable in the Variations of the middle movement. The orchestra used is the classical combination employed by Beethoven: strings, wood-wind in pairs, the usual brass, and timpani.

The *First Symphony*, Op. 26, is on a larger scale, having six movements, the last requisitioning two solo voices and a full chorus. The orchestra shows an inclination to groups of three in the wood-wind. There are 3 Flutes, 3 Clarinets, 3 Trumpets; but only 2 Oboes, 2 Bassoons, and 4 Horns. There is also a new feature, which does not appear in the Concerto—a desire for vitality of tone texture, shown in the opening *tremolo* for the strings (an improvement on Wagner's tremolo), in the trills and runs in the final movement, and in the further division of the strings. Occasionally, however, he only succeeds in keeping the parts busy. The string parts in the second movement are very fine, and he already reveals a fondness for the clarinet as a solo instrument, a preference which never left him. He has once for all relieved his violoncellos from the rather insignificant task of supporting the double-basses. He is at no loss to find numerous alternatives for obtaining the eight-feet tone—in the timpani, the bassoons, the tuba, or even by dividing the double-basses themselves in octaves. On the other hand, one of the chief characteristics of this Symphony is the number of fine singing melodies which he frequently gives to the double-basses and violoncellos. He already reveals a strong liking for themes on the horns, in one place marking them naïvely *pavillon en l'air* (bells held up). In the vivid colouring of the 9–8 *Vivace,* we see the influence of Taneieff and Tchaikovsky. There is plenty of light and shade in the contrasts, and sufficient cohesion in the balance of tone. In his *Tutti,* he rarely gives the bass notes to the cellos, thus obtaining a greater sonority from the stringed orchestra. The harp is introduced in the *Finale,* just before the entrance of the voices. We shall refer to the choral writing later on.

The *Second Symphony* also opens with a slow movement. A similar orchestra to that of the *First Symphony* is used, but the harp is not requisitioned. There is a firm advance in the handling of the instrumentation which points to a close study of Dvorak's work.

For the *Divine Poem* (Third Symphony) the orchestra is much larger and the instrumentation more advanced.

Piccolo.	3 Trombones.
3 Flutes.	Tuba.
3 Oboes.	Timpani.
English Horn.	2 Harps (separate parts).
3 Clarinets.	16 First Violins.
Bass Clarinets.	16 Second Violins.
3 Bassoons.	12 Violas.
Double Bassoon.	12 Celli.
8 Horns.	8 Double Basses.
5 Trumpets.	

The orchestration throughout is rich, sonorous, well-balanced, and effectively coloured.

The modern harmony of the *Poem of Ecstasy*, Op. 54, rightly demands a modern colouring; and the orchestration is accordingly modern in texture and hue. The "wind" section is exceptionally rich, being laid out in groups of threes. The English Horn and the Double Bassoon are also used. There are 5 Trumpets in B flat, 8 Horns, 2 Harps, and a wealth of percussion—Cymbals, Triangle, Gong, Small Bells (*Clochettes, Campanelli*) needing two players, Large Bell (*Grande Cloche, Campana*), and Celesta. A Solo Violin and a Cello play important *rôles* in the opening *Lento*, and the Organ enters at the climax in the *Finale*. The "string" section is much subdivided, and both the violins and the cellos have very brilliant parts.

Elaborate as the orchestra is in the *Poem of Ecstasy*, we find Scriabin making even greater demands in his next score, *Prometheus*. Here is the orchestra :

Colour-Organ.	Triangle.
Piccolo.	Small Bells.
3 Flutes.	Large Bells.
3 Oboes.	Celesta.
English Horn.	2 Harps.
3 Clarinets in B.	Organ.
Bass Clarinet in B.	Piano.
3 Bassoons.	Sopranos.
Double Bassoon.	Altos.
8 Horns in F.	Tenors.
5 Trumpets in B.	Basses.
3 Trombones.	First Violins.
Tuba.	Second Violins.
Timpani.	Violas.
Bass Drum.	Violoncellos.
Cymbals.	Double Basses.
Gong.	

Prometheus can be performed without the Colour-Organ and without Chorus. For the *Campanelli* (little bells) two players are necessary. The *Cam-*

panelli parts are written an octave lower than the real sound. The Celesta part likewise. The large bells are to be tuned—Tenor D, E, G, A, C.

The orchestration of this tone-poem is of the most advanced and modern character of any orchestral work ever written. The piano plays an important *rôle,* having many of the leading themes, but it is at the same time a constituent part of the whole scheme. The handling of the orchestral colour is masterly in the extreme. There is nothing approaching it even in Schönberg, Stravinsky, or Strauss. Alike in the gloomy, vague, and nebulous atmosphere of the opening, where sustained *tremolos* for muted strings, with long-drawn notes for muted horns, and the roll of drums suggest things immaterial and shadowy, through all the varied phrases of the development, right up to the magnificent climax of intense effulgence and quivering light, we feel almost stunned at the composer's wonderful mastery over musical sounds and tone-colours. Nowhere is there any such tone-picture of dazzling light and radiant colour.

In comparison with the modern works of Strauss, Scriabin's orchestra, even for *Prometheus*, seems almost what we term classical. Compare it with the following orchestra of Richard Strauss :

4 Large Flutes.	2 C Clarinets.
Piccolo.	2 A Clarinets.
4 Oboes.	4 Bassoons.
Heckelphone.	Contra Bassoon.
E flat Clarinet.	8 Horns.

4 Trumpets.	20 First Violins.
4 Trombones.	20 Second Violins.
Bass Tuba.	12 First Violas.
8 Drums (two players).	12 Second Violas.
Triangle.	10 First Cellos.
Bass Drum.	10 Second Cellos.
Organ.	12 Double Basses.
12 Trumpets (off the stage).	

and the use of the aerophor, a mechanical bellows for sustaining notes on the wind instruments; and all this huge array and panoply for one of the most bombastic sound pieces ever written, the *Festival Prelude*, for the opening of the Vienna Concert Hall in 1913.

Although I have included in the heading of this chapter the term "vocal writing," the use of the voice plays an extremely small part in the huge musical output of Scriabin. The voice really made very little appeal to him, and I think his case must have been still more extreme than that of Beethoven, who, whenever he conceived a melody or a subject, always heard it on an instrument, and never on a voice. The only two examples of his vocal writing are used as adjuncts to his orchestral works—the Choral Prologue to his *First Symphony* being as ordinary and old-fashioned as the vocal ending to his *Prometheus* is advanced. The Fugue in the *First Symphony* is little more than a "school work," very regular and proper in form, and thoroughly diatonic in style; whilst the choral part in *Prometheus* has a close relation to the "Three Nocturnes,"

Nuages, *Fêtes*, *Sirènes*, of Debussy. The choralists do not sing words, but merely vocalise mystic sounds, such as, ah-oh-a-ee. Their part is an exceedingly unvocal one, and, I should imagine, would be almost impossible to sing without the support of the organ, which seems to be supplied in the score merely for that particular purpose.

XVI

THE SOURCES OF HIS INSPIRATION

THE fortuitous nature of the appearance of Russian works in England is responsible for many erroneous, and even unfair, opinions concerning the work of many of the Russian composers. The greatest factor in the English enlightenment as to Russian musical art was the Beecham Russian Opera and Ballet Season of 1911. Then for the first time a really representative series of great Russian works was given with Russian singers and conductors, including the great basso, Chaliapin.

At an earlier date the appearances of the Symphonies of Tchaikovsky and other Russian composers, under the baton of Henry J. Wood at the Queen's Hall, London, have been rather on the "inverted cone" principle, but felicitous nevertheless; Tchaikovsky was not the typical Russian, like Mussorgsky, Borodin, Rimsky, and others; and if his last Symphony, the *Pathétique*, was the first to be heard in London, and the others came in retrograde order, it mattered little in his case, for he had not the continual and perfectly progressive and evolutionary genius of Scriabin. But to commence with Scriabin's *Divine Poem*, to follow it with his *Prometheus,* and not to know the First and Second Symphonies at all, nor the *Poem of Ecstasy,* was a course which could hardly produce a proper impression of Scriabin's music and aims.

It is always fascinating to trace the origin of a composer's musical creations. Purcell and Handel, Beethoven and Brahms, all found their chief inspiration in the natural scenes of the country which they loved so much; Schumann and Schubert found their inspiration in literature (and what poor sloppy literature it was occasionally!); Wagner, McDowell, and Vaughan-Williams derived their musical impetus from the SEA—that symbol of the vague longing and unrest which is the life-force of the world.

Few writers, however, have noticed that one of the chief inspirations in music comes from MUSIC itself. All the greatest composers founded their work on that of the past masters, and this not only in matters of technique and construction, but in the essential idea itself. What Handel tried to tell us about Nature in the Pastoral Symphonies of his Organ Concertos, thousands of others have tried to do in later times in different ways.

This pensive semi-philosophic mood is a great feature in Scriabin's music. The Russian tone-poet derived much also from Wagner, Liszt, Chopin, Schumann, even César Franck. This is not to disparage him in the least. All great people act similarly—and must do so. The hearing of great music suggests to original minds that they can carry the same idea to a higher (or a deeper) power, and they do it. This explains much music which the superficial critic merely passed off as "reminiscent in mood." Scriabin's closest mood-affinity is undoubtedly with Chopin. The loftiness, the poetry, the exquisite finish of artistry, and the patriotism of the great Pole were, as it were, but the mirror of his own temperament.

Both, too, were great lovers of nature. As a boy Scriabin's holidays were all spent in the country. He loved to dream there for hours together, and was very sensitive to the beauty of clouds and of flowers. When Joseph Hoffmann was on tour in Switzerland, a musician came to him after one of his recitals and said: "Whenever I hear Scriabin's E flat *Prelude* from Op. 11, I have a clear vision of huge rocks rent asunder. I wish I knew what he had in his mind when he wrote it." Hoffmann forgot the incident till some months later, when he met Scriabin in Petrograd, and chanced to play him the Prelude in question. "Do you know how I came to write it?" asked the composer. "I was standing on the bridge at the Bastel in Switzerland, looking down at the flashing torrent flowing between the great rocks it had torn asunder in its course, when the idea came to me." This derivation of Music from NATURE persisted all through his life. When in Moscow nearly half the year was invariably spent in some distant province in the country; and almost all his music was conceived there, although some of the bigger works were finished on his return to the city. Like Mr. Stephen Graham, the famous English tramper in Russia, the spirit often drove him into the wilderness, to the mountains and valleys, by the side of the great sea, and to the haunted forests. Once the vast dome of heaven became the roof of his house, there he re-found his God, and his being re-expressed itself in terms of eternal Mysteries.

What the Rhine was to Beethoven, the Volga was to Scriabin. "Great Mother Volga" he knew in all her many moods and passages. Dr. Bury writes: "I have always understood the strong appeal to the historic, and even the poetic sense which the Rhine puts forth, but I have never understood the sense of the Ideal which a great river might convey until I saw, approached, and crossed the Volga." If a prosaic English Bishop can be so moved by the mere sight of the Volga, how strong must have been the influence of this wonderful river on Scriabin, who knew all her reaches intimately! . . . More than any other country, Switzerland moved him to musical recording, and it was there his wonderful feeling for Light and Colour made itself felt and grew until it became finally the main idea in his music. The same force which made Milton a visionary made Scriabin a mystic. Both saw the fullest manifestation of the Creator's glory most beatifically in the endless wonders of LIGHT and SOUND.

> "Who by His all-commanding might
> Didst fill the new-made world with LIGHT."

The glowing Dante-like canvases of the sixteenth-century Puritan became vague, often nebulous, but no less glorious, visions with the twentieth-century

Moscovite seer, who was a true-blooded representative of that strange land of twilight and vivid colours, of Western science and Eastern mysticism, of exotic culture, with its vivid native imagination and love of beauty.

It is not the sunset—that symbol of the dreamer—much less the moonlight and gloom (so beloved of the French musicians); but rather the glory of the rising sun, the majesty of morning *crescendo*, and the full blaze of noon, which we find in his music. Like Ruskin, he is a lover of the clouds, of the tops of mountains—and of soliloquies. All this acted and reacted on his music, which became more and more visualised. Not only the interior world is reflected in his pieces (for Art with him is always the Expression of Inner Truths), but he also reproduces the actual spectacle of things. In this derivation of musical harmony from the LIGHT and COLOUR of Nature, he was on very much safer ground than he was later on, in the actual combination of Colour and Sound in *Prometheus*. In many of the pieces of his early and middle periods we find the souvenirs of days and journeys, of scenes visited and mental experiences; obviously he was *visibly* inspired by nature. If Scriabin saw God Immanent so clearly in the book of Nature, he saw God transcendently in this World of Light and Sound. With him we are indeed brought near to the Infinite, and we do indeed "gaze across the cloudy elements into the Eternal Sea of Light." Physical and sensuous art it may often be. Yes, but always deeply spiritual as well. "Other-worldliness" is the key-note of his work. In the shorter pieces, the Prelude, etc., of his latter periods he may be almost entirely occupied with the physical side of the beauty of Light, and his symbolic indications may appear unnecessary.

The lines of Swinburne come to mind :

> "All lutes, all harps, all flutes, all lyres
> Fall dumb before Him e'er one string suspires,
> All stars are angels, but *the Sun is God*."

In his longer pieces—the Sonatas, the Symphonies, etc.—we find him grappling seriously with world problems and spiritual forces. In his last Sonatas he is indeed endeavouring to pierce the great truths—the wonder of Birth itself, the mystery of Death, the unending puzzle of the ultimate Destiny of the worlds. And he does everything through a glowing harmonic sheen of continually changing beauty and light.

This brings us to another source of Inspiration to Scriabin—his connection with Theosophy.

And this is where I am very much at sea. I am not a Theosophist, and cannot "function on the astral plane," as they put it. Scriabin would hardly expect one to judge of Theosophy by his music. Still less is one able to estimate his music in terms of Theosophy. I am keenly sympathetic and appreciative of Scriabin's outlook in life and art ; I can at any rate judge of the effect of Scriabin's music on myself, and Scriabin certainly wrote his music for the general public, and not for the Theosophists in particular.

I can well imagine that when Scriabin joined the

Theosophists he would eagerly welcome a system of Philosophy which fitted in so well with what musicians are ever trying to express more clearly. For no philosophy has systematised the scale of the emotions—that region so vaguely treated by Spencer and all the others—so well as have the Theosophists. Nor does any other system approach so closely to the regions of that "sixth subconscious sense"—indefinable though undeniable—upon which music operates chiefly. Theosophists occasionally seem to give too much play to the life of the senses; but one can see at once why a musician could welcome such a philosophy, for it appears to explain much which he is trying to understand.

Scriabin claims that his theosophy grew out of his music. I think he was mistaken here. I can readily imagine that many things in Theosophy stimulated his musical imagination in many new and more forceful ways. During the last forty years theosophic circles, small but select, have sprung up in most of the large cities in Europe. Important groups were formed in London, Berlin, Brussels, Paris, and many other places. But particularly in Russia has the new cult taken root amongst what are known as the "intelligentsia." There are ten Universities in Russia, the smallest of which has over a thousand students. Both Moscow and Petrograd have close upon ten thousand. Over 40,000 men are training for professional careers, 15,000 law, 10,000 science chemists, etc., 10,000 medicine, and comparatively few for teaching.

Free-thinking in Russia can only take certain non-political lines, and one which has proved attractive to many of these young thinkers is the connecting up of Religion, Life, and Art. The Established Churches had not met their requirements. Some sought new sensations; others, a simplification of life and a repose of soul; others wished to associate religious aspiration and social ideals by giving both a religious basis. Theologians and poets are seldom musical. The former repress emotion, good and bad, and devitalise the senses until they are scarcely allowed to function at all; the latter are ever jealous of a medium so closely allied to their own, and only allow a union of their words with music with reluctance. Men of science (especially chemists) and painters are invariably musical; and medical men are now becoming awake to the therapeutic uses of Music. Much nonsense has been written about the close connection of Music and Religion in the Western Churches, but this is seldom proved in practice, for the general run of Church music is of so poor a type as to be quite negligible in this respect.

Scriabin always held the highest view of his art. No one was freer of self-seeking and of worldliness, no one so inflexible in pursuing his ideal. Here then was a possible union of Religion and Music which appeared to him ideal. Here at any rate was an exercise of the religious faculty which gave a prominent place to Art, Beauty, and Design, and which seemed to have disappeared in religious art after the period of the great cathedral builders.

The young Russian is, as Stephen Graham puts it, "interested in God." Someone has described Russian Religion as a "holy love"; the Roman Religion as a "holy fear." Be that as it may, Theosophy secured a considerable footing in Moscow, Petrograd, Charkoff, and other Russian cities amongst the younger thinkers.

Theosophy is defined as the science of religions; it embraces all, but this embrace has apparently failed on account of its very hugeness, and the philosophy which should cover all has frequently become a special cult of its own.

East and West, despite Kipling, do decidedly seem to meet in this new cult; and the commingling of two great racial forces is well illustrated in Theosophy, which as a cult resolves itself into a curious blend of Christianity and Pantheism. The Christian believes in a God Immanent and Transcendent—God in us, around us, and above us. The Buddhist believes in a God Immanent but not Transcendent—in everything but not outside of everything—and looks forward to a time when his existence will be merged finally in Nirvana.

How does Scriabin apply all this to his music? The composer is apparently striving to obtain by means of his music that state of ecstasy which the true mystic realises can only be obtained when a perfect union with the divine has been achieved. As regards his pianoforte music, even the Sonatas—this attitude is hardly convincing. Occasional indications of the style of the music are put in

French; but by any other names, his music would sound as sweet.

He chooses to call his favourite chord, built up by fourths, the "Mystic Chord," but there is no mystery—except that of Musical Sound itself. Rather, it is severely logical. The only case in which we can seriously consider his combination of Theosophy is in his *Prometheus;* and there it has provided the tone-poem with a strong story or "programme." For the rest, it will, and must be, heard as music *per se.* In his *Mystery*, sketched out just before his death, he was to carry on the combination to a rite, in which the performers were to take a passive part. But we cannot discuss this, as, although the whole scheme was in Scriabin's mind, hardly anything was committed to paper.

Undoubtedly theosophic ideas helped Scriabin much with his inspiration, but they are certainly not very apparent, much less obtrusive, in most of his creations. The later pieces are wonderful creations in the world of sound. Enjoy their marvellous beauty, whilst philosophers wrangle over the aim of beauty. The Sonatas are great works of art developed with perfect finish. Everyone will read their own programme into them. I have already referred to this in Chapter X in the case of the *Fifth Sonata*.

Art as Religion, and Religion as something involving the conception of Art is the fundamental idea of Scriabin's music. His first Symphony is a "Hymn of Art," and joins hands with Beethoven's *Ninth*. His Third, the *Divine Poem*, expresses the spirit's liberation from its earthly trammels and the consequent free expression of purified personality; whilst his *Poem of Ecstasy* voices the highest of all joys —that of creative work. He held that in the artist's incessant creative activity, his constant progression towards the Ideal, the spirit alone truly lives. In *Prometheus* he reaches the furthest point of his ecstasy in creative energy—a point which was to have been carried astoundingly further by his proposed *Mystery*, in which Sounds, Colour, Odours, and Movement were to be united in expressing one fundamental religious idea.

This attempt to secure a clearly defined connection between Art and Religion is not confined to Music. That brilliant Russian actress, Vera Kommisarzhevskaia, had the same restless searching genius, "the perpetual longing, the strange religious craving" that possessed the great Russian writers. She too attached great importance to colour-schemes—to half-mystic utterances and pregnant silences as with that other mystic, Maeterlinck.

Painters too, like Ivanoff, had their gaze turned in the same direction. This artist's sketches and studies show a wealth of ideas no less astounding than his originality of method. Like Vrubel, later on, he approaches a novel world in which Oriental mysticism is allied to the early Christian art of the old Russian Iconographers. Apropos of this, Dr. R. R. Terry has pointed out the relationship of Scriabin's new musical method to the old Mediæval system of music. Other musicians besides Scriabin have worked on similar lines, but none so characteristically and persistently as Scriabin. If we admit this attempt at combining Theosophy and Music, then Scriabin has been far more successful than Wagner in his *Parsifal.* But the novelty of the position is open to challenge. With Michelangelo the sculptor, Leonardo da Vinci the sculptor, Beethoven the musician, just as with the English Watts and Tennyson, Art and Religion were undeniably coupled. So with Scriabin, it is sufficient for the hearer to accept roughly a philosophic and religious basis without any clearer definition of designation. Indeed this attitude towards his music seems to be the one desired by Scriabin, the elaborate explanation of whose music is due to his followers rather than to the composer himself.

All these artists and thinkers then are linked together in a movement which is the national reaction to that gross materialism which of late has been weighing so heavily on governments and individuals alike, almost to the point of complete asphyxiation.

In this light, Scriabin's music is of inestimable value at the present time. I know of no music so entirely spiritual as that of Scriabin; none so entirely sincere or self-effacing—although often so difficult of approach for the performer. His music is the exact antithesis to the terrible realism of modern German and Italian composers, and the weird productions of the Florentine musical Reformers—who, as Professor Hadow says, " in order to add a new page to music hold it necessary to tear out all the other pages."

. . . . . .

There are other influences which appear only occasionally, but these are mostly in the earlier works. That of the Russian Church scales may be found in many of the early Preludes; and the Folk-song evidently plays some part in the composition of the Concerto and the Symphonies, although no actual folk melodies are used.

. . . . . .

In conclusion, I feel that this is the least satisfying portion of the book, which, however, was only embarked upon mainly to set out Scriabin's life and creations. I would recommend those who wish to pursue this line of thought further, to read the Gifford Lectures [1] (1914) of the Right Hon. Arthur James Balfour, especially the one on *Æsthetic and Ethical Values.* As to the origins of the real musical thought, of which sounds, technique, and the canons of the art are but as the veil, this is a region which even metaphysicists and psychologists have not yet been able to approach, much less to enter.

[1] *Theism and Humanism,* A. J. Balfour (Hodder and Stoughton, 1915).

XVII

SCRIABIN'S POSITION IN MUSIC

Few will deny to Alexander Scriabin the designation of Modernist; many may bestow on him the somewhat dubious appellation Ultra-Modernist. It matters not. Modernity is no new thing. In its best sense, it is nothing more than "present-dayism," and viewed in this light, it is as old as the hills. Modernism was known to the Egyptians, and was a favourite topic with the ancient Greeks. It was discussed in the Roman forums, and doubtless agitated the early cuneiform draughtsmen. Modernity is certainly not confined to any one nationality. This adventurous spirit has always been present in music, and indeed it is the spark which makes for vitality and progress in all the arts and sciences alike. There is hardly a single great work of music which was not greeted with opposition at first. Indeed, many of the greatest geniuses in music had to encounter lifelong opposition. Wagner in his *Music Drama* writes that nothing irritates self-satisfied criticism so much as a steadfast faith. Certainly Bach's career was no exception. The life of this great genius was one long story of petty bickerings with little Jacks-in-office; and even after his death, his great *St. Matthew Passion* was left entirely forgotten until Mendelssohn revived it nearly a hundred years after its composition. Even Handel's music,[1] which was as simple as Bach's was complex, was often hissed and booed by his spiteful enemies. Gluck, the great opera Reformer, was the subject of endless cabals; whilst the engaging Mozart had his health undermined by the cold reception of many of his greatest works. It was the same with Beethoven. Lord Lytton, writing in the *Fortnightly Review* in 1872, speaks of a musician of Beethoven's day once describing his sensations in listening to the great C minor Symphony. He was "one of the three," he said, "who sat to the end of the Symphony *out of respect for Beethoven*."

Indeed the whole story of musical evolution from the early days of Claudio Monteverde up to our own time, anything that is new and unusual in art, has always excited envious and malicious attacks. And certainly Alexander Scriabin's experience was no exception to the rule.[2] But our audiences are now growing much less narrow-minded, and even in the professional ranks, where the opposition usually is much keener, a modified attitude is becoming much more usual. No art can stand still. We move in swift times; and new phases of art and thought appear with every new moon. A multiplicity of styles is one of the most striking characteristics of

[1] His *Messiah* met with much opposition in London on its first performances in 1743 and 1745.

[2] The musicians in the orchestra "struck" at his mild *tremolo* for the violins, saying it was not possible. Evidently "strikes are not of modern invention."

modern art. To say that one does not understand the new music is not the same thing as calling it bad music. If we do not know a man's speech and musical idioms we cannot rightly judge his works. Of course, all is not music that is modern; nor is all good that is old. There is such a diversity of style about modern art that a keen observer has remarked that each succeeding new style is shorter in duration than the one before it. Even if some of the newer tendencies do seem at first sight like a bird alighting from a resting place only to fly away again out of sight, yet they do leave their impress on the art. The plan of labelling the different styles rather confuses than helps. People mean different things by the same terms. The "Futurist" of the Florentine School headed by Marinetti, is mixed up with the so-called French "Impressionists," and are not clearly distinguished from the Franck-d'Indy schools, and so on.

Terms are employed as if they were of universal validity in literature and other arts, having absolutely no meaning when applied to music. Phrases like "Romanticism," "Classicism," "Materialism," and "Impressionism" have no relevance to the musical art. For music has no element of copying nature, like art. It stands by itself, self-supporting, self-sufficing.

The most interesting personalities in music—the English: Cyril Scott, York-Bowen, Vaughan-Williams, William Wallace; the Hungarian: Bartok; the Russian: Rébikoff and Scriabin—defy classification. The "whole tone" scale, for instance, is not a purely French device; it was reached on other lines by Schönberg; and (as we have shown) Scriabin arrived at it through a purely scientific channel.

It is only natural that worn-out conventions should be assigned to the rubbish heap. An element of adventure and experiment will always form some part of evolution and progress in art. The wise wonder at the usual; the unwise at the unusual. All this does not mean a complete breaking with the past. Far from it; for every new delight I find in modern music, a deeper appreciation of the older (the best of it) is begotten.

Modernity reveals itself in two ways in music:

(*a*) by texture, style of handling, or whatever you please to call it.

(*b*) by the subject-matter or the thought itself.

Scriabin is an extremist in both these ways. In the texture and the style of his later period he demands a new language, a new scale, a new way of listening and of composing. One of the vital questions in musical progress is the problem of Discord; it is almost as elusive and perplexing as the problem of Pain in Theology. The standard of æsthetics varies from age to age. A combination of notes which one generation accepts only on sufferance will be received by a later generation with equanimity or even with delight:—Monteverde's Sevenths, Wagner's Ninths, Gounod's Thirteenths, Debussy's Twelfths, and so on. Scriabin's system of harmony founded on fundamental scientific laws of vibration opens the door for every possible progression of intervals. All the pedagogic accumulation of harmonic lore of the last two hundred years may as well be scrapped. Many passages in Scriabin's work seem ugly to us—some almost repulsively so. The presence of the offensive kinds of ugliness in art is the penalty society pays for treating Art as negligible. It is the fruit of lack of understanding. Whatever people who are devoid of artistic sense may say, mankind cannot do without Art; and it often takes its revenge remorselessly for being slighted. Mankind is mirrored in his arts in his baser as well as his finer qualities. The uglinesses which represent fine qualities are welcome, and the uglinesses which represent incompetence, insincerity, stupidity, cunning, greediness, narrow-mindedness, and such unfortunate obliquities reveal to us things we could very willingly do without—though we are quite aware that we never shall.[1]

Then, as to matter, Scriabin is essentially what writers of the last generation used to call *fin-de-siècle.* The attempt to bring Art, Religion, Philosophy, and even Science into closer relationship is not confined to any particular nationality. We see it in England with Thompson and Graham, in Sweden with Ibsen and Strindberg, in France with Maeterlinck; experimenters all—but significant. It is the natural reaction of deep thinkers against all that has become conventional, meaningless, hollow, in established religion, politics, and social order.

In Russia, that Country of Extremes, we find the symptoms very marked. Scriabin took his music boldly over into the theosophical tracts; Rébikoff's

[1] Sir Hubert Parry, *On Ugliness in Art.*

music concerns itself with sociological subjects; Stravinsky's ballets and tone-poems with ethnology. But I do not think Scriabin was any more successful than the others in this direction. As with the actress, Kommisarzhevskaia, her special art became in danger of suffocation from the unallied forces introduced. Scriabin was in my opinion misled by that interesting but unfruitful peculiarity of music from the philosophic point of view, which is, that it of all the arts seems to be more intimately connected with dry scientific facts. You can state in terms of mathematical physics certain very important truths with which music is intimately connected, and at first sight it seems as if science was going to give assistance in building up a theory of musical æsthetics. Mr. Balfour gave it as his opinion in 1911 that the belief of any possible connection would prove illusory. Scriabin's *Prometheus* has gone far to prove that something of the nature of a true musical æsthetic can be deduced out of the mathematical theory of scales and chords, or of the theory of harmony.[1]

Successfully or otherwise, the daring revolutionary genius of Scriabin has tested this connection to the *n*th power, and quite apart from their intrinsic value his works will always remain a brilliant exposition of the possibilities of these lines. Such an exploration could not possibly be effected without opening up other long vistas of wonderful possibilities. Whilst the other Russian composers have

[1] Right Hon. Arthur J. Balfour. Report of International Congress of Music, 1911, Novello.

been experimenting in many other altogether different ways—Akimenko, with his Russo-French methods; Rébikoff, with his psychosociology; Glazounoff and Liadoff, with their Schumannesque puzzles—a little naïve; Stravinsky, with his quintessence of primitive folk feeling, and so on—Scriabin has opened up an entirely new territory, and, like Wagner, has exploited it himself to the utmost capacity. It may be a brilliant failure in a way, and yet it is a masterly success. It did not lead Scriabin to the goal he was seeking, and I think his proposed *Mystery* would have led him on to still more impossible ground.

His *Prometheus* means, once for all, a withdrawal of mathematical and acoustic theories from practical harmony, which must ever remain in the sphere of æsthetics alone.

His union of Light and Sound too has not, nor will not, pass the stage of an interesting experiment. What are we to say then of Movement and Heat? The best conjunction so far is the Russian *melomimique*, which constitutes a far more artistic blend than words, music, and action in the opera. In his peculiar outlook on life, religion, and art Scriabin remains essentially a Russian of the Russians. In his musical achievements he has left a contribution to instrumental music worthy to rank with any of the great masters of the past—Bach, Mozart, Beethoven, Brahms, and Chopin not excepted. His bold attack on routine proves to the hilt that the codes of the art could undergo a complete æsthetic renewal without owing anything to official and academic encouragement. His fecundity, his courage, and his sure originality have struck a severe blow on academic convention, and have wrested from the academics the prestige of teaching which has lain so heavily on the students of the last fifty years, conventions transmitted from master to pupil without consideration for the evolution of modern life or for the growing intelligence of the auditor. In fact Scriabin has brought about a *complete renewal of the hearing faculty which will fertilise not only one field, but the whole of the musical art.*

XVIII

FUTURE POSSIBILITIES

> *"La musique est si jeune encore qu'elle ne connaît pas sa force, qu'elle ne soupçonne pas sa puissance."*
> *Saint-Saëns.*

WHEN we consider that Music, as we Westerns understand it, is the youngest of all the arts, barely three hundred years old, its amazing development, slow in the seventeenth century, more sure in the eighteenth, and nothing short of marvellous in the nineteenth, we are dumb with amaze at the future possibilities of the tonal art. "Music in our day," writes William Wallace[1] (the only living direct descendant of the great Wallace), "consists of a perpetual struggle to give definite expression to subconscious thought. No one can tell for how many centuries the strife will continue until man evolves the new faculty which will make the content of music clear. Whatever it may signify in time to come, we are bound to consider it as a faculty fitted to the special circumstances of him who possesses it. In remoter times man may have heard, with the ear of his mind, all that was necessary for his life and for his way of living. The faculty for music has gradually developed in step with human needs

[1] *The Threshold of Music* (Macmillan and Co).

and endeavours. It is now, more than at any former period, seeking for a substantial basis upon which to erect itself in closer relation with the other expressions of man's mind. It has a vague perception that its destiny is yet to be pronounced, and those who possess it are showing this by their work. We are all groping in a mist, and the sum of our life is but a breath tossed to the wind. But, if the history of evolution is of any value, surely we who employ the musical sense are the forerunners of a race which will bring into man's comprehension a new form of reason—perhaps even an altered system of ethics."

Is further progress possible upon the lines laid down in Scriabin's new harmony? Not, I think, with the method used by Scriabin. His effort to catch a higher mystic meaning naturally involved him in innovation and experimentation, which led to an exaggerated (perhaps even a false) use of his chords. This was brought about by his extended mystic ideas, and the idea of combining Sound and Colour. This certainly crippled his melody, and led him occasionally even to meaningless repetition and reiteration of his points, which stood in the way of sustained development and phrasing. His curious, almost anxious, devotion to exact design also exaggerated this defect; for instance, he frequently repeats the last bar of a three-bar phrase, apparently merely for the sake of a poetical balance.

But on other lines undoubtedly his exploitation of the higher harmonies will lead to wonderful developments, which are even already in evidence. Certain passages in the music of York-Bowen, Frank Bridge, John Ireland, and many other English composers go far to point the way.

Scriabin's adoption of the "raised eleventh" (or 4th), particularly with his absolutely free treatment of inversion and spacing, is especially stimulating. But his habit of altering it at will into a "diminished twelfth" (or fifth) is open to question. The net result of his developments points in the direction of the adoption of a "tertia-tonal" system—the division of the octave into 18 steps. Then indeed would still more wonderful harmonies be possible, and these on a system of tuning much more perfect than the present one. Wisdom, discovery, art, science, civilisation have all risen in the East and set Westward in ebb and flow. Will Music again ebb Eastward before its next stride forward in energy and expression and development? The great Italian pianist and composer, Feruccio Busoni, thinks so, and looks forward to a tertia-tonal scale system. The famous musical theorist, Dr. Menchaca of Buenos Ayres, urges a much finer system of musical tuning; and the Italian composer, Aleleona, has written music for an even more delicately divided octave.

The question of concord and discord in musical art may be raised here; but after all this is but a school quibble, for there is no hard and fast line between the two. The older contrapuntists reckoned the "fourth" as a discord. Nowadays we accept the dominant seventh as a concord; and then comes Scriabin with his wonderful structure of fourths, which he accepts as the most perfect of concords, and this latter position is absolutely necessary for the full comprehension of his later works.

As for his proposed union of sound and colour, music does not stand to gain much by it; *rather is it likely to lose.* Even the question of opera, where words, music, and acting are combined, has not yet reached a satisfying art form. One cannot even watch the wonderful Russian ballets without missing much of the splendid music which was specially written for them. The boundaries of an art are never widened by alliance with a sister art. I have recently been shown a book on textile weaving from musical notation.[1] Music has not gained thereby, and I have not yet heard of any wonderful development in the ancient art of pattern weaving resulting therefrom.

One is reminded of that pluralist, who is becoming rather fashionable at our cathedrals just now, the priest-organist. He is usually either a poor priest or a poor organist, occasionally both.

So it is with the union of the arts. One tends to lose much; but frequently *both* are the poorer thereby.

[1] *Harmonic and Keyboard Designing.* An easy method of producing an endless variety of most beautiful designs suited to numberless manufactures by unskilled persons from any piece of music, by C. H. Wilkinson, author of *Harmonious Colouring.*

POSTSCRIPT

THE early works of Scriabin were engraved in Russia some twenty-five years ago. They are not very well done, and are not free from the misprints which mar the copies of his work throughout his life. The full scores of all his orchestral works were engraved in Germany and are beautifully done. Owing to the unsatisfactory condition of the international copyright laws in Russia—indeed there are none—this plan of having his works engraved outside the country is the only possible way for the author to secure the copyright, and enjoy the proceeds of his works.

The later works were all engraved in Moscow and are done in a highly finished way which it would be difficult to surpass in any country. But all the copies, right from the early to the final period, contain serious misprints, not easy for the uninitiated to discover quickly; and this is all the more serious with music of so original (and at first strange) a character as Scriabin's, not to mention the difficulties of the new notation. I intend to take an early opportunity of publishing a complete list of these musical *errata*.

APPENDIX I

SYMPHONIES AND SONATAS

1. *Pianoforte Concerto*, Opus 20, written about 1894 whilst a student at Moscow. First performed about 1896. Full score published by Belaieff in 1898.

2. *Reverie* for orchestra, Opus 24. Written whilst a student at Moscow. Full score published by Belaieff in 1908. Pianoforte duet arrangement by A. Winkler.

3. *First Symphony*, Opus 26, in E major with Choral Epilogue, written about 1895 whilst a student at Moscow Conservatoire. Performed about 1897. Full score published by Belaieff in 1900. Pianoforte duet arrangement by A. Winkler published in the same year.

4. *Second Symphony*, Opus 29, in C minor. Composed at Moscow some time before 1903. Full score published by Belaieff in the same year. Arrangement for two pianofortes by B. Kalafaty in the same year.

5. Third Symphony, *The Divine Poem*, C minor and major, Opus 43, written in the summer of 1903 probably in Switzerland. Full score published by Belaieff in 1905. Pianoforte duet by Léon Conus published in 1908.

6. *The Poem of Ecstasy*, Opus 54, finished in January, 1908, at Lausanne. First performed at Moscow 1909.

Awarded the Glinka prize in 1909. Full score published by Belaieff in 1908. Pianoforte duet by Léon Conus in 1908.

7. *Prometheus*, or *Poem of Fire*, begun at Brussels in 1909, finished at Moscow April, 1910. First performed at Moscow March 2, 1911, under Kussevitzsky. Full score published by the Russian Musical Publishing Society in 1911. Arrangement for two pianos by Léon Sabanieff in 1913.

Pianoforte Sonatas

First Sonata, Opus 6, in F minor, written at Moscow in 1892, immediately at the end of his student's course. Published by Belaieff in 1895.

Second Sonata, Opus 19—*Fantasy Sonata*—in G sharp minor. First movement written at Genoa in 1892, second movement written in the Crimea in 1897. Published by Belaieff in 1898.

Third Sonata, Opus 23, in F sharp minor, written on the Maidanoff Estate in 1897. Published by Belaieff in 1898.

Fourth Sonata, Opus 30, in F sharp major, written (probably at Moscow) in 1903. Published by Belaieff in 1904.

Fifth Sonata, Opus 53, in F sharp major, written at Lausanne in 1908. First published at his own expense in Paris in the same year. Published later by the Russian Musical Publishing Society.

Sixth Sonata, Opus 62, in G. Started at Beattenberg in 1911, and finished a little later. Published by the Russian Musical Publishing Society in 1912.

Seventh Sonata, Opus 64, in F sharp, written at Beattenberg in 1911, finished before the *Sixth*. Published by the Russian Musical Publishing Society in 1913.

Eighth Sonata, Opus 66, in A. Written at Moscow in the early part of 1913. Published by Jurgenson in 1913.

Ninth Sonata, Opus 68, in F, written immediately after the Eighth. Published by Jurgenson in 1913.

Tenth Sonata, Opus 70, in C, written in Moscow immediately after the Ninth. Published in Moscow in 1913.

APPENDIX II

THE COMPLETE WORKS

Written when a Young Boy

(Published by Jurgenson, Moscow)

Op

1. Waltz in F minor.
2. (i) Etude; (ii) Prelude; (iii) Impromptu à la Mazur.
3. Ten Mazurkas (2 Books).

Works of Student Period

(Published by Belaieff)

Op.

4. Allegro appassionato. 1894.
5. Nocturnes: (i) F sharp minor; (ii) A major.
6. Sonata No. 1, F minor.
7. (i) Impromptu à la Mazur, G sharp minor; (ii) F sharp minor.
8. Twelve Etudes.
9. Prelude and Nocturne (for the left hand only).
10. Two Impromptus.

FREE PERIOD (1893 TO 1897)

Op.
11. Twenty-four Preludes.
12. Two Impromptus.
13. Six Preludes.
14. Two Impromptus.
15. Five Preludes.
16. Five Preludes.
17. Seven Preludes.
18. Allegro de Concert, B flat minor.
19. Sonata-Fantasia No. 2, in G sharp minor.
20. Pianoforte Concerto in F sharp.
21. Polonaise in B flat minor.
22. Four Preludes.
23. Sonata No. 3, in F sharp minor.
24. Reverie for Orchestra.
25. Nine Mazurkas.
26. First Symphony.

TUTORIAL PERIOD

(Moscow Conservatoire: 1897 to 1903)

Op.
27. Two Preludes: (i) G minor; (ii) G major.
28. Fantasia in B minor.
29. Second Symphony in C minor.

FREE PERIOD (1903 ONWARDS)

(All published by Belaieff)

Op.
30. Sonata No. 4, in F sharp major.
31. Four Preludes.
32. Two Poems.

Op.
33. Four Preludes.
34. Poème Tragique.
35. Three Preludes.
36. Poème Satanique.
37. Four Preludes.
38. Valse in A flat major.
39. Four Preludes.
40. Two Mazurkas.
41. Poem, D flat major.
42. Eight Etudes.
43. Symphony No. 3 in C (*The Divine Poem*).
44. Two Poems.
45. Three Pieces.
46. Scherzo.
47. Quasi Valse.
48. Four Preludes.
49. Three Pieces: (i) Etude; (ii) Prelude; (iii) Reverie.
50. Missing.
51. Four Pieces.
52. Three Pieces.

Works Published by the Russian Musical Publishing Society

Op.
53. Sonata No. 5.
54. Le Poème de l'Extase.
55. Missing.
56. Four Morceaux: (i) Prélude; (ii) Ironies; (iii) Nuances; (iv) Etude.
57. Two Pieces: (i) Désir; (ii) Caresse Dansée.

Op.

58. Feuillet d'Album (New Russian Album, Vol. I).
59. Two Morceaux : (i) Poème ; (ii) Prélude.
60. Prometheus.
61. Poème Nocturne.
62. Sonata No. 6.
63. Two Poems : (i) Masque ; (ii) Etrangeté.

FINAL WORKS PUBLISHED BY P. JURGENSON, MOSCOW

Op.

64. Sonata No. 7.
65. Trois Études.
66. Sonata No. 8.
67. Deux Préludes.
68. Sonata No. 9.
69. Deux Poèmes.
70. Sonata No. 10.
71. Deux Poèmes.
72. Vers la Flamme. Poème.
73. Deux Danses : (i) Guirandes ; (ii) Flammes Sombres.
74. Cinq Préludes.

APPENDIX III

NOTES ON THE COMPLETE PIANOFORTE WORKS

Op. 1. *Waltz in F minor.*

A work of his studentship period. Well finished but not characteristic, except for bars 26 and 58, where he shows a liking for striking harmonic clashes.

Op. 2. *No.* 1. *Etude C sharp minor.*

Also a work of the student period. Very Chopinesque.

Op. 2. *No.* 2. *Prelude B major.*

A sweet little miniature.

Op. 2. *No.* 3. *Impromptu à la Mazur.*

Chopinesque; note the harmonic clashes at bars 25, 45, etc.

Op. 3. *Ten Mazurkas* (*in* 2 *Books*).

Ten pleasing dance pieces of no great individuality, sometimes peculiarly Chopin-like, occasionally Schumannesque, and at times rather commonplace.

Op. 4. *Allegro appassionata.*

A good concert piece with evidences of Liszt's influence; it was originally conceived as part of a Sonata.

Op. 5. *Two Nocturnes.* No. 1, F sharp minor. No. 2, A major.

Two charming pieces rather Chopin-like, but containing many interesting touches. Notice the original harmony at bar 56 in No. 1, and bar 25 in No. 2.

Op. 6. *Sonata No.* 1, *F minor.*

A brilliant *Allegro*, an expressive *Andante*, and an effective *Presto* broken into by a Funeral March and an Angelic Hymn. The gloom at the end is thrust aside impatiently by the determined motive notes, which Scriabin frequently uses in the same way as Beethoven with his " Knocks of Fate."

Op. 7. *Two Impromptus à la Mazur.* No. 1, G sharp minor. No. 2, F sharp minor.

The first of these shows little advance on any of the preceding works, but the second is much more characteristic both in the harmonic and the rhythmic treatment, sets of four notes in the bass being crossed by sextolets in the treble.

Op. 8. *Twelve Etudes.*

An exceedingly fine set of mood pictures, making considerable technical requirements. The F sharp minor *Capriccio* was a great favourite with the composer, as was likewise the *Alla ballata* in C sharp minor, and the pathetic D sharp minor, No. 12, with its fine rich chords. No. 10 in major thirds is significant of the composer's restless searching into harmonic feeling.

Op. 9. *Prelude and Nocturne* (*for the left hand only*).

Two exceedingly fine pieces which many players will be quite willing to play with both hands in order to secure the full musical charm from them.

Op. 10. *Two Impromptus.* No. 1, in F sharp minor. No. 2, in A minor.

The first contains a beautiful hymn-like melody for the second subject. The second is not very characteristic.

Op. 11. *Twenty-four Preludes.*

These Preludes are much shorter than the *Etudes*, Op. 8. They are arranged so as to pass through a circle of 24 keys, from C major, through the sharp keys and back again through the flats. The minor coupled up to the major is always the one related by key-signature. Many of these little miniatures are of great value to the pianist. They were written at widely different times.

Op. 12. *Two Impromptus.*

The first piece is rather of the Etude order, a very melodious *Presto*, and in Scriabin's favourite key, F sharp major. The Second Impromptu is very poetic, and the Coda points to the immense sonority of the *Fantasia*, Op. 28, and the later Sonatas.

Op. 13. *Six Preludes.*

The first of these is a remarkable piece which has the calm religious feeling of Bach. It might well have been inspired by some old Church chant. No. 3 is a delightful miniature, whilst No. 6 is merely Schumann-esque.

Op. 14. *Two Impromptus.*

Two graceful sensitive pieces, the last containing another of Scriabin's famous hymn-like melodies.

Op. 15. *Five Preludes.*

The first is rhythmical, the second and third demand great stretching powers for both hands. Most of the work in No. 4 goes to the left hand. The fifth is not very characteristic.

Op. 16. *Five Preludes.*

No. 1 is of great beauty, but the extended arpeggios of the left hand require very delicate handling. No. 2 is massive in its harmony. No. 3 is a moonlight scene, whilst the fourth piece is almost unique in its simplicity and its use of the three-bar theme. No. 5 has much charm. This is a very attractive set.

Op. 17. *Seven Preludes.*

The technique is much further advanced in this set, both from the player's and the composer's point of view.

Op. 18. *Concert Allegro in B flat minor.*

A fine concert piece which demands wrists of steel for its performance. A very beautiful second subject.

Op. 19. *Sonata-Fantasia No. 2, in G sharp minor.*

A very poetical and expressive *Andante* with a turbulent *Presto* which contains, however, a singing subject of great beauty.

Op. 21. *Polonaise in B flat minor.*

The only example of Scriabin in this form. Not a very attractive piece.

Op. 22. *Four Preludes.*

The first is very beautiful and quite naturally ends with a half-cadence. The second and the fourth are of little value, and contain many misprints. The *Allegretto*, No. 3, is very charming.

Op. 23. *Sonata No. 3, in F sharp minor.*

The culminating point of the composer's first period. It has a strong psychological programme.

Op. 25. *Nine Mazurkas.*

Very interesting specimens of the dance element in Scriabin, the spirit of which he derived from Chopin. The last is particularly characteristic.

Op. 27. *Two Preludes.*

No. 1 is very poignant in its grief-laden phrases. It is given *in toto* by Corder in his *Musical Composition* (Curwen), as a striking instance of Scriabin's abundant and original use of the "French sixth" chord, and his curious round-about resolutions of passing-notes. Corder says the laying out of this piece is wellnigh perfection. The second, *Andante*, has a deep poetic charm, and is very daring in harmony.

Op. 28. *Fantasia in B minor.*

One of Scriabin's finest pianoforte pieces, full of wonderful themes, strong in development, and brilliant in texture.

Op. 30. *Sonata No.* 4, *in F sharp major.*

A direct forerunner of the *Poem of Ecstasy*. Leading themes are used to represent Aspiration and Languor. The characteristic chord of the *Poem of Ecstasy* is also found in this Sonata. The orgiastic coda, which is a feature of all his later works, is already present here.

Op. 31. *Four Preludes.*

The first is a charming *Andante* with a cross-rhythm arpeggio in the bass. Although marked *Andante* it is metronomed at 50 to the crotchet. Most of Scriabin's *Andantes* are *Lentos*. The piece is a curiosity inasmuch as it begins in D flat and ends in C major. The augmented eleventh is already in use (bar 27). There is a very Chopin-like touch at the cadence. The Second Prelude, marked *Con stravagante*, is in what Beethoven would have called his " unbuttoned " mood; it is fierce and aggressive. The Third Prelude is more of the nature of a short Etude. It is a study in quintoplets. This superb set concludes with one of those perfect little harmonic miniatures which only Scriabin wrote.

Op. 32. *Two Poems.*

A pleasing piece in Binary form. The first subject is Chopin-like, the second one, marked *Inaferando*, more characteristic. Both subjects in their turn are considerably elaborated. The Second Poem is full of rich chords.

Op. 33. *Four Preludes.*

A very attractive set; the first very serene; the second meditative, marked *Vagamente;* the third, stormy; and the fourth, Etude-like.

Op. 34. *Tragic Poem.*

Full of massive harmony, it owes much to Liszt. The sharpened fifths in the chords of the ninth should be noticed.

Op. 35. *Three Preludes.*

This set has been weakly described as Chopin, Wagner, and Schumann. Appropriate as the first may be, the second contains too much characteristic feeling to be thus lightly passed over.

Op. 36. *Poème Satanique.*

In this piece, Scriabin is supposed to hint at the evil forces which oppose the soul in its evolution to the fulfilment of its highest aspiration. The themes show some relation to those of the *Poem of Ecstasy*. In this piece, the harmony has been carried yet another stage further.

Op. 37. *Four Preludes.*

The first two are Chopin-like in character, whilst the last two are Scriabin himself, one in his contemplative mood, a slow *Andante;* the other is an angry outburst. There is an highly original chord in the penultimate bar.

Op. 38. *Valse in A flat major.*

This piece was at one time much favoured by the composer. It is of the salon order, the right hand weaving all sorts of rhythmic patterns over a regular left-hand beat. The piece is of considerable length; it has a presto coda and pianissimo ending.

Op. 39. *Four Preludes.*

No. 1 is a sound and pleasing *Allegro;* No. 2 owes something to Wagner, but more to Scriabin himself. No. 3 in its *Languido*, and No. 4 with its strong chords, are entirely Scriabinic.

Op. 40. *Two Mazurkas.*

No. 1 is one of the most charming dance pieces of Scriabin. It has a strong relationship to the *Caresse Dansée*, Op. 57. There is a striking shifting of the tonality at the end. The melody in No. 2 is thrown into the tenor register and requires very deft handling.

Op. 41. *Poème, D flat major.*

A very beautiful melody with an intricate accompaniment figure.

Op. 42. *Eight Etudes.*

A fine set of rhythmical studies:—the first, nine notes against five; the second, three against five; the third, running in *Prestissimo* triplets; the fourth and fifth are more of the Prelude order; whilst the sixth returns to combined rhythms (five against three), with a superimposed melody; very difficult; the seventh, three against four (much easier); the final one returning to five against three. This last, with its fine interlude of solid harmony, is perhaps the most popular one in the set.

Op. 44. *Two Poems.*

An attractive melody over a gently undulating accompaniment to which the second number forms an admirable contrast.

Op. 45. *Three Pieces.*

A meditative Album-leaf, a fantastic Poem of considerable interest in relation to Scriabin's later harmony and a very effective Prelude. This is one of the most popular sets of pieces.

Op. 46. *Scherzo.*

A fine harmonic piece in 6–8 time of the *Presto* order.

Op. 47. *Quasi Valse.*

Another of Scriabin's interesting excursions into the dance form with modern harmony. The progression of the diminished fifth in the bass should be noticed.

Op. 48. *Four Preludes.*

An exceedingly characteristic set. The first is a fiery impetuous *Allegro;* the second, a poetic meditation of great delicacy; the third, an agitated *Capriccioso* spread out arpeggio-wise; the fourth, a festive and radiant March, despite the triple time.

Op. 49. *Three Pieces.*

An *Etude* like an Æolian harp, a brusque and angry *Prelude* with fierce drum beats in the bass, a *Reverie* of exquisite fineness make a charming set.

Op. 50. *Missing.*

Op. 51. *Four Pieces.*

Fragilité is a tenor melody accompanied by limpid treble chords with triplet arpeggios in the bass—an entirely characteristic piece. So too is the lugubrious prelude in A minor and the expressive "poem of wings." The languid dance at the end is likewise characteristic. All four are quite short.

Op. 52. *Three Pieces.*

A Poem of great charm based on a new harmony, an Enigma based on the winged soaring figures, and a Languid Poem—all three characteristic, and acceptable.

Op. 53. *Fifth Sonata.*

A one-movement piece based on the following motto:

I call you to life, O mysterious forces
Submerged in depths obscure
Of the Creator-Spirit, timid embryons of life,
To you I now bring courage.
(*Poem of Ecstasy.*)

Op. 56. *Four Pieces.*

An aggressive Prelude, almost savage in its power; an ironic *Scherzo* with some delightfully tender harmonies in the contrasted phrases; a soft velvety movement entitled *Nuances*, and an airy *Etude* which might well be called a Dance of Sprites. The first, third, and fourth are quite short, the second rather longer.

Op. 57. *Two Pieces.*

The first (a page long), entitled *Désir*, contains some wonderfully expressive harmony. The second, a charming *Caresse Dansée*, is one of his most characteristic pieces of the dance order.

Op. 58. *Album-leaf.*

This is issued only in the *Russian Composers' Album* by the Russian Musical Publishing Society. It is a slow meditation of exceedingly delicate harmonic texture. The key-signature is now abandoned on account of the new harmony.

Op. 59. *Two Pieces.*

Two pieces, both in the composer's advanced style. The Poem, a graceful and sweet *Allegretto*, meditative in mood; the Prelude, one of Scriabin's most aggressive and defiant outbreaks.

Op. 60. *Prometheus.*

The pianoforte part to this orchestral poem is published separately, but gives no indication of the orchestral parts. A proper idea of this work can only be obtained on the keyboard by the arrangement for two pianos (four hands).

Op. 61. *Poem-Nocturne.*

One of his most important pieces. The technique is already in advance of his *Prometheus*, and probably points forward to the style projected in the *Mystery*. There are many indications that the composer had ideas in his mind which are not definitely conveyed by the music.

Op. 62. *Sixth Sonata.*

The key-signature has been abandoned since Op. 58. Although composed as "absolute" music there are many indications such as "the dream takes shape," etc., which point to a psychological basis for this Sonata, which is filled with the tolling of bells and ends in the deepest gloom.

Op. 63. *Two Poems.*

The first *Masque* is full of quaint harmonic patterns, the second *Etrangeté* graceful and sweet and very modern in feeling. The English pianist, Mr. Leonard Borwick, has a particular liking for these two pieces.

Op. 64. *Seventh Sonata.*

The mystic element in Scriabin's music here reaches its apogee. This Sonata was called by its composer a White Mass, as opposed to the Ninth Sonata, which he styled a Black Mass. It has many strong points much in common with *Prometheus*, and points forward at the same time to a proposed *Mystery.* Some huge spiritual conflict is being waged in this piece.

Op. 65. *Trois Etudes.*

These Three Studies present difficulties to the player, notably the first one, in which the right hand fantastically runs along in ninths throughout. In the second *Allegretto* the melody is doubly lined-out in sevenths. The third, which runs along in fifths, is much more playable and taking, having a striking contrasted theme of much power.

Op. 66. *Eighth Sonata.*

Like all the other Sonatas of the third period this composition, the longest of all Scriabin's works, is founded on one of the so-called mystic chords. The harmony is very remarkable; there are two long development sections, and we have the usual ecstatic vertiginous coda in dance rhythm.

Op. 67. *Two Preludes.*

We here reach a stage in Scriabin's harmonic development which may be called the fourth period, a style which points forward to his proposed *Mystery* rather than backward to his *Prometheus.* No piece is more typical of this new phase than this vague, mysterious and harrowing first Prelude, the sorrow-laden strains of which form such a striking contrast to the second piece, a *Presto,* full of strange quivering light.

Op. 68. *Ninth Sonata.*

One of Scriabin's most pessimistic works. The element of the diabolical enters largely into it, and it was called by the composer a " Black Mass." I append a verse of Hardy's as a description of this gloomy piece.

" Last as first the question rings
Of the Will's long travailings;
Why the All-mover,
Why the All-prover
Ever urges on and measures out the droning tune of Things."

Op. 69. *Two Poems.*

The first is a fragile and tender meditation, *Allegretto* in C, based on the C chord as Scriabin imagines it. The second a dreamy *Andante* of great sweetness.

Op. 70. *Tenth Sonata.*

One of Scriabin's most optimistic works, full of radiant light and colour. One might very suitably quote another verse from Hardy's *Dynasts :*

" But a stirring thrills the air
Like to sounds of joyance there
That the rages
Of the ages
Shall be cancelled, and deliverance offered from the darts that were.
Consciousness the Will informing, till It fashion all things fair ! "

The characteristic harmony tends to a process of simplification, and the usual method of classical development is reversed inasmuch as the themes, instead of expanding, become more and more concentrated and abbreviated.

Op. 71. *Two Poems.*

The first, a fantastic piece, contains many real harmonic derivatives. There are some very novel chords containing strident semitonic clashes. The tolling of bells relates it closely to the *Eighth* and *Ninth Sonatas.* Some annotators have distinguished two distinct phases in this direction, that of harmony proper, and that of *timbre* or *clang*, the latter playing a great part in Scriabin's last period.

Op. 72. *Towards the Flame.*

This poem is one of the most important of all Scriabin's pieces; advanced in harmony, it is thoroughly radiant and luminous. In colour and mood alike, as well as in its triumphant ending it is closely allied to *Prometheus.*

Op. 73. *Two Dances.*

In these two dances, *Garlands* and *Dark Flames*, we have strong mystic elements which render the meaning very obscure.

Op. 74. *Five Preludes.*

This final set of Scriabin's pieces is very striking. The harmony is such that some of his most enthusiastic followers have refused to go thus far with him. The mood of the first is sad, even heart-rending. No. 2, contemplative; No. 3, tragic; No. 4, vague, indefinite, contemplative, but not pleasing; whilst the final one is proud and warlike, with a remarkable ending.

APPENDIX IV

APPROXIMATE PRONUNCIATION OF THE RUSSIAN NAMES MENTIONED IN THE TEXT

Akimenko . .	Ak-ee-main-koh.
Arensky . . .	Ahr-rain-skee.
Asanchevsky . .	Ah-san-chev-skee.
Belaieff . . .	Bay-lah-ee-ef.
Borodin . . .	Bor-oh-deen.
Bortniansky . .	Bort-nee-an-skee.
Cui . . .	Quee.
Dargomijsky . .	Dar-goh-mee-ee-skee.
Glazounoff . .	Glah-zeu-noff.
Glière . . .	Glee-yair.
Glinka . . .	Glee-nk-ah.
Gogul . . .	Go-gul.
Grechaninoff . .	Gret-chan-ee-noff.
Pavlova . . .	Pahv-loh-vah.
Ivanoff . . .	Eev-an-off.
Kommisarzhevskaia .	Kommisar-shevs-kah-yah.
Kussevitzsky . .	Kooz-say-vit-skee.
Liadoff . . .	Le-ad-off.
Medtner . . .	Maid-t-ner.
Mussorgsky . .	Mooz-sorg-skee.
Nietzsche . .	Nee-aits-chay.

Obmana . . .	Ohb-mah-nah.
Pushkin . . .	Poosh-kin.
Rachmaninoff . .	Rach-mah-ne-noff.
Rébikoff . . .	Raib-ee-koff.
Rimsky-Korsakoff .	Reem-skee-Kor-sak-off.
Safonoff . . .	Saf-oh-noff.
Scriabin . . .	Scree-ab-in.
Stravinsky . .	Strah-veen-skee.
Taneieff . . .	Tahn-nay-ee-eff (very quick and smooth).
Tchaikovsky . .	Tchah-ee-kov-skee.
Zieke . . .	Zee-ek-kay.
Zviereff . . .	Tsvee-air-eff.

INDEX

Printed in the United States
143396LV00003B/91/A